MEDITERRANEAN DIET COOKBOOK

How to Get Started with the Mediterranean Eating to Live Healthier, Lose Weight with Easy & Delicious Recipes and a Meal Plan for Beginners to Kickstart Your New Lifestyle

Includes a 60- DAY No-Stress Meal Plan

By
Lizzy McFields

By choosing to use eco-friendly paper for this book, we are making a conscious effort to be as environmentally sustainable as possible. Not only are you getting a great read, but you're also supporting sustainable practices with your purchase.

Copyright© 2022 Lizzy McFields - All rights reserved. Edition 2023.

ISBN 979-8362197766
10 9 8 7 6 5 4 3 2 1

Book Editing and Proofreading by C.T.
Book Design, and front Cover Design by E.T. Design

Socials:
Facebook Page: @LizzyMcF
Facebook Private Group: Lizzy McFields Publishing
Instagram: lizzy_mcfields_publishing
Amazon Author Page: Lizzy Mcfields
Email: info@lizzymcf.com

GET YOUR BONUS NOW!

Hello Fantastic Reader!

First, I would like to thank you for purchasing this Cookbook. I am sure it will be beneficial to improve your knowledge about this diet, especially your eating habits and overall well-being!

To prove my gratitude and appreciation for your trust in my scientific experience, I am happy to gift you with my "Whole Body Reset Diet Book" and my food diary, "Daily Food Journal," which I am sure will make your health explode by tracking your daily progress. Don't wait any longer. Follow the instruction below to receive the digital copy for free! Enjoy your reading!

We're sorry if you come across any editing errors in the book. Please report them to *info@lizzymcf.com* and any new ideas to improve the structure and information in the book. Please, include the title of the book in the email object. To thank you for your time, we would like to offer you the opportunity to receive all our new releases. Thank you for being so cooperative with my team and me.

This bonus is **100% free**, with not string attached.
You don't need to enter any detail except your name and email address.

To download your bonus scan the QR code below

Table of Contents

Close your eyes and imagine you are on the coast of Tuscany on the Mediterranean Sea. You are on a seaside terrace sitting at a table with a classic blue tablecloth that echoes the colors of the sea's surroundings. The water reflects the warm rays of the day's sun in a beautiful cloudless blue sky. The restaurant waiter the meal you requested with a big smile while the smell of food and salt water makes you feel relaxed and at peace with the world. From below comes a voice: it is that of a fisherman who has just caught fish talking to the farmer who is bringing the brightly colored vegetables he has just harvested to the restaurant.

Open your eyes: now, you can recreate this magical place in your kitchen and enjoy these delicious, fresh, easy-to-prepare foods typical of the Mediterranean Sea.

I have Italian roots on my maternal grandmother's side. The recipes in this book were savored in her places of origin and then reproduced in my kitchen in San Francisco to be tested and selected in a place away from Italy and the blue zone countries to collect them in this book.

You can taste these wonderful places right in your kitchen through the flavor of these recipes.

But beyond taste, there is more! Remember that the Mediterranean diet has immense benefits. In recent years, much research has been conducted that has shown that people living near the Mediterranean Sea are healthy and long-lived compared to people living in other parts of the world. They enjoy a better quality of life and health despite their advanced age. This happens because people living near the Mediterranean Sea have a healthy lifestyle, as well as the food they eat. But not only that-they, but they also play sports every day! How? They ride bicycles to move short distances and walk a lot.

They eat preferably locally grown foods and cook extra virgin olive oil; they often accompany their meals with a good glass of red wine, eating in company. Moderation in the amount of food is the key to a successful diet, and in the Mediterranean population, this is an inherent characteristic. Year after year, the Mediterranean diet is ranked as the best, becoming increasingly popular.

As already pointed out, the key is healthy food and moderation. It is, in fact, a balanced diet, rich in variety, making it nutritionally balanced and healthy.

When people come to me for help, I always recommend following my systematic dietary approach applied to the Mediterranean Diet as an essential and starting principle if there are no particular diseases. The balance and nutrition offered by the Mediterranean Diet perfectly meet needs as varied as weight loss, treatment of heart disease or diabetes, or simply general health and well-being.

This diet is not only healthy, but it is also easy to follow. The main rule, as in any other healthy diet, is to eliminate foods that are highly processed, contain hydrogenated fats, and are full of excess sugar. It is a very varied diet that pleases all tastes; it includes slow-release unprocessed carbohydrates, healthy fats from olive oil, nuts and seeds, lean proteins, and lots and lots of vegetables and fruits.

Many people today have already decided to eat this way, but it is still essential to learn how to adjust portions of each type of food to meet your individual needs, and this can be very easy with the food guide I will show in this book. If your body is used to carbohydrates (perhaps in combination with an aerobic sport), you can eat a little more. If you feel better with more fat, no problem: add more foods rich in unsaturated (healthy) fatty acids consumed in moderation instead of saturated ones.

When you try these recipes, they will not only make your taste buds explode with flavor, but your body will feel rejuvenated with more energy and, most importantly, be healthier. Remember that you can have a healthier and longer life as early as today, thanks to the Mediterranean diet. Embrace the diet and lifestyle of the Mediterranean peoples today!

Let's start cooking together!

THE SCIENCE BEHIND THE MEDITERRANEAN DIET

The Mediterranean diet has emerged as an original prototype for current dietary claims in the United States and other countries. It has been internationally recognized. Let's look at some of the definitions given for this diet: the first was by Willett et al. (1995) The latter stated that the Mediterranean diet (MD) reflects the typical dietary patterns of some areas of Italy and Greece in the early 1960s, where adults' life expectancy was remarkably high. Rates of diet-related chronic diseases were low.

Since the early 20th century in the United States, it has been documented that the satisfying flavors, and thus high acceptability, of the Mediterranean diet offer opportunities for dietary improvements, such as increased consumption of fresh fruits, vegetables, and grains. Extra-virgin olive oil is a key ingredient for its many antioxidant properties. Significant immigrant populations to the United States from Greece, Italy, and Spain have helped raise awareness of the Mediterranean style of eating in the United States.

The Mediterranean food model is currently included in the 2020-2025 version of the Dietary Guidelines for Americans. It is considered a substitution of the U.S.-style healthy nutritional model, based on the types and proportions of foods typically consumed in the United States, albeit in nutrient-dense forms and adequate amounts.

A simple way of eating that relies on whole foods, especially vegetables, seafood, and healthy fats, has long been a part of Mediterranean countries and cultures.

Unlike other diets that emphasize calorie counting and avoidance of certain foods, the Mediterranean diet is about enjoying more fresh ingredients and meals prepared from scratch as much as possible. Tips also include enjoying meals with friends and family.

References:
Willett WC, Sacks F, Trichopoulou A, Drescher G, Ferro-Luzzi A, Helsing E, Trichopoulos D. Mediterranean diet pyramid: a cultural model for healthy eating. Am J Clin Nutr. 1995 Jun;61(6 Suppl):1402S-1406S. doi: 10.1093/ajcn/61.6.1402S. PMID: 7754995.

PRINCIPLES OF THE MEDITERRANEAN DIET

Unlike the typical American diet, the Mediterranean diet is high in fiber and low in saturated fat. As you will see below, the overall fat content of the Mediterranean diet is not necessarily low. In any case, the fats promoted in the Mediterranean diet are "healthy" monounsaturated fats, such as those found in olive oil, which does not raise cholesterol levels. A "classic" Mediterranean diet is unavailable, as many countries bordering the Mediterranean Sea, so the Mediterranean diet varies. However, the American Heart Association reports that traditional Mediterranean diets include:

• Moderate to high levels of fish and moderate levels of dairy products (mainly cheese and yogurt.)
• Beans.
• Fruits, and veggies.
• Unrefined cereals
• Wine.
• A high level of olive oil.
• Low intake of meat and meat products.

The following table shows the amount of each dietary groups included in the Mediterranean diet, based on a daily intake of 2000 calories.

NUTRIENTS	AMOUNT
Fish/Seafood (Protein)	23-68g (0.8 – 2.4 oz)
Dairy (Protein and Fats)	250-525g (1 – 2.1 cups)
Fruits (Fiber and sugars)	175-300g (1.4 – 2.5 cups)
Vegetables (Fiber)	108-369g (1.2 – 4.1 cups)
Oils (Fats)	19 – 40 g
Grains (Carbohydrates)	57-153g (2.0 – 5.4 oz)
Meat & Poultry (Protein)	99-102g (3.5 – 3.6 oz)
Added sugars	24 g

People living in different regions of the Mediterranean basin have different food styles and preferences. The fresh ingredients available are not the same from one area to another, but they share the basic principles of the Mediterranean Diet.

One common aspect of all these people is that their diets are mostly plant-based. The ingredients used to create meals are seasonal, fresh, and locally sourced. The focus is on unprocessed foods, including whole grains, fresh fruits, and vegetables. The main source of added fats is olives, through extra virgin olive oil, while other healthy fats come from fish, nuts, and seeds. Dairy products are consumed in moderation, focusing on fermented products such as cheese and yogurt. Red meat and red wine should be consumed in moderation but are still part of the diet.

These common dietary guidelines bring to the table all the best that nature has to offer. When we eat according to these principles, our bellies will be full, and our bodies are well-nourished, alongside the pleasant taste of what we eat.

MODERATION IS ALWAYS THE MAIN KEY OF A DIET SUCCESS

In the Mediterranean Diet, everything is allowed, even sweets, to a small extent. But only in moderation. The people of this region know that the excess of a good thing (mainly containing simple sugars) is bad for your health. This applies to good foods as well. Overeating (many calories) causes weight gain and disease, even if the calories come from healthy foods.

FOODS FRESH AND IN SEASON

When you consume fresh, seasonal produce, you maximize the nutritional intake of these foods. The less time that passes between harvest and consumption, the better. The nutritional value of plant foods begins to decline as soon as they are removed from the soil or plant on which they grow. It is even better if they come from local sources and have not had to spend time in storage or transit. The healthiest ones are organic because some farmers use pesticides anyway. Generally, it is good to know that the more time it spends out of the soil or plant before being eaten, the more nutrients are lost. Ideally, you should grow your vegetable garden (if possible).

EATING PLANTS IS IMPORTANT

Vegetables, fruits, legumes, grains, nuts, and seeds form the basis of the Mediterranean diet. At least three-quarters of your plate will be filled with plant foods. They are rich in fiber, vitamins, minerals, and phytonutrients, all of which have health and disease prevention benefits.

VEGETARIAN MEALS

Legumes, such as beans, lentils, and chickpeas, are often used as a plant-based protein source. They are incredibly versatile because they can also be paired very well with protein foods of animal origin, such as tuna (a "classic plate" is tuna, beans, and onion). They can be used in pasta dishes, stews, and soups or pureed to make sauces and creams, such as hummus. They are a source of low-GI carbohydrates, protein, and soluble fiber. They help control blood sugar levels and reduce the risk of colon cancer and cardiovascular disease. In short, they have a lot of beneficial properties.

If you like these nutrients, you don't have to limit yourself to consuming them only twice a week; follow the nutritional table below in the following chapters to have a complete diet and include them effectively in your nutritional table. Start experimenting with our tasty legume dishes if you are unfamiliar with them. You can soak them and cook them from scratch, but canned options are just as good and much faster to prepare. In the latter case, just remember to rinse them well to remove the salt.

BIOCHEMICAL PROCESS SUPPORT

They are involved in extracting energy from the food we eat, strengthening the immune system, and controlling inflammation in the body. Micronutrients also help lower blood pressure and reduce the risk of cancer.

WHOLE GRAINS SHOULD BE YOUR CHOICE

Unprocessed whole-grain carbohydrates provide energy to the body through starch, vitamins and minerals, and soluble and insoluble fiber. Whole grain pasta, couscous, barley, bulgur, and polenta are commonly used in Mediterranean cooking. They take much longer to digest than refined carbohydrates. They are released more slowly into the bloodstream through glucose, causing a slight increase in blood sugar levels and a reduction in insulin levels. It has long been shown that including whole grains in the diet reduces the risk of obesity, heart disease, some cancers, and type 2 diabetes. Choose stone-ground or type 2 flour whenever possible.

FATS CAN BE HEALTHY

Monounsaturated fats are found in olives, olive oil, avocados, pears, oily fish, nuts, and seeds. They offer protection against heart disease by lowering total and LDL cholesterol levels and increasing HDL cholesterol levels. Monounsaturated fats have anti-inflammatory properties, which help control chronic inflammation caused by many health conditions, including obesity, dementia, and arthritis. Most of the fat in a Mediterranean-style diet comes from foods rich in these essential fats.

PREVENT CONSTIPATION EATING FIBER

Fiber slows the release of blood sugar, helping to control blood sugar levels and prevent the onset of type 2 diabetes. Cholesterol is bonded by soluble fiber, thus preventing its absorption into the bloodstream. It therefore, helps to lower blood cholesterol levels and prevent heart disease.

FISH IS AN IMPORTANT SOURCE OF PROTEIN

Let's address the issue of protein. Regarding animal protein sources, oily fish is the centerpiece of the Mediterranean Diet. Bluefish have dark fat veins (brown in general), such as tuna, trout, salmon, sardines, and mackerel. White fish, such as halibut, hake, sole, or whiting, are also important protein sources. Including fish in your menu at least twice a week is essential. Oily fish, in particular, is an excellent source of omega-3 fatty acids, which help reduce cholesterol levels and protect the body from inflammation.

CHEESE AND YOGURT INTAKE NEED TO BE MODERATED

Small portions of cheese and yogurt are included in the Mediterranean diet. Milk is not routinely consumed in this region, but a small number of fermented products are consumed daily. This can be a little Greek yogurt for breakfast and a small portion of cheese as a snack or to flavor a salad. Why fermented? Fermentation makes these products gentler on the digestive system, reducing the amount of lactose present. They also provide a source of beneficial bacteria, which promote gut health. A healthy gut has been shown to have benefits for the entire body. Excessive weight gain/loss is linked to an unhealthy gut, type 2 diabetes, heart disease, brain functioning problems, depression, and anxiety. This diet keeps the metabolism active so that you have the right balance.

YOU CAN ENJOY WINE

If you like to have a glass of wine with a meal, you can continue by choosing red wine. Wine is rich in polyphenols, but it is not an essential Mediterranean diet component. You do not have to start drinking it if it is not for you. Red wine contains antioxidants that reduce the body's inflammation processes and the risk of heart disease.

RED MEAT IS TO LIMIT

Very little red meat is consumed in the Mediterranean diet or small amounts if it is part of a meal. Red meat contains a lot of saturated ("bad") fat, so it is necessary to decrease the amount of red meat consumed. Saturated fats are the building blocks that go on to form cholesterol. Although a certain amount of cholesterol is needed in the blood to produce hormones and other structures in the body, excessive consumption has been linked to heart disease such as stroke.

HEALTH BENEFITS OF THE MEDITERRANEAN DIET

Recent nutritional studies on the health benefits of the Mediterranean diet apply a score that compares an individual's intake of food groups or nutrients with the median intake of the study population. The Mediterranean diet scores high on this scale because it includes higher median intakes of vegetables, fruits, nuts, legumes, whole grains, and fish, and lower median intakes of red and processed meats, moderate alcohol intake, and a high ratio of monounsaturated to saturated fats, in many cases, also reducing dairy products. In most studies, individuals who followed a Mediterranean diet presented a reduced risk of cardiovascular disease, a lower incidence of cardiovascular disease, and an overall lower mortality rate (Guasch-Ferré M et al., 2018; Davis et al., 2015).

LONGEVITY

The Mediterranean Diet reduces overall mortality by about 10%. Genetic, environmental, and lifestyle factors mainly determine the lifespan of humans. The Mediterranean and high-quality diets (such as the anti-inflammatory diet) are associated with a reduced risk of all-cause mortality (Ekmekcioglu, 2019).

You can also consult my other cookbook, "Anti-inflammatory diet Cookbook" (available on Amazon), to combine the two diets.

HEART DISEASE RISK REDUCED

According to the AHA (American Heart Association), the Mediterranean diet ranks first in preventing heart disease. The incidence of major cardiovascular events is reduced by the Mediterranean diet, thanks partly to the use of extra virgin olive oil and nuts, which contain "good" fats. This diet can help lower blood pressure, decrease the risk of heart attack and stroke, and reduce inflammation in the arteries, which is essential because clogged arteries, or atherosclerosis, are the leading cause of death in the United States. The diet promotes the consumption of lots of fruits and vegetables and limits the consumption of red meat. The diet also focuses on fresh, natural ingredients with more vitamins and minerals than processed foods. These factors result in a diet rich in heart-healthy nutrients and low in saturated fats and added sugars (Gantenbeinet al., 2021).

MOOD AND DECREASES STRESS ARE REDUCED

Many studies have shown that following the Mediterranean diet can reduce the risk of depression and improve mood. How is this possible? Well this diet encourages a lifestyle that moves away from hectic and stressful Western activities and focuses more on family, exercise and reducing time spent on media devices. It encourages meals with family and friends, daily physical activity incorporated into everyday activities, and an active lifestyle. These factors can improve mood and overall mental health (Sánchez-Villegas et al., 2013).

EASY DIGESTION

Fiber is a key part of your diet, along with anti-inflammatory properties and nutrients that work as pre and probiotics, creating a more diverse gut microbiota and improving bowel function. Changes in the gut microbiota are correlated with health status. Data from the literature on gut microbiota show that all dietary changes can alter the gut microbiota composition. The Mediterranean diet is associated with reduced all-cause mortality. Evidence suggests that the Mediterranean diet modulates gut microbiota, increasing diversity. A Mediterranean dietary pattern is associated with specific characteristics of the gut microbiota. Evidence suggests that the gut microbiota of subjects following a Mediterranean diet is significantly different from that of subjects following a Western dietary pattern. The latter show increased intestinal permeability, which is responsible for metabolic endotoxemia (Merra et al., 2020).

BLOOD GLUCOSE LEVELS UNDER CONTROL

Various studies have shown that the Mediterranean diet reduces the risk of diabetes. It can be used as a preventive diet for type 2 diabetes because of its low-carbohydrate elements. This diet is rich in fiber, which is digested slowly and prevents glycemic surges by promoting intestinal motility. By balancing the consumption of simple carbohydrates (the sugars found naturally in fruits and dairy products) with complex carbohydrates such as whole grains, proteins, and healthy fats, digestion can be slowed down enough to utilize the carbohydrates and adequately reduce insulin resistance. This can also help maintain a healthier weight, as obesity triggers diabetes (Mirabelli et al., 2020).

WEIGHT CONTROL

The Mediterranean diet encourages eating quality meals instead of a quick bite. It spurs taking a walk to the nearest grocery store instead of driving, reducing portion sizes, and eating slowly instead of eating too fast. Combined with the best variety of nutrients and reducing saturated fat consumption, these factors can help you healthily lose weight and maintain a healthy diet.

INFLAMMATION REDUCED

Chronic inflammation is the main culprit of many diseases. These include cardiovascular diseases, digestive disorders, joint pain, and more. Omega-3 fatty acids have been shown to reduce inflammation. The Mediterranean diet includes foods rich in omega-3 fatty acids, such as salmon, tuna, walnuts, and chia seeds. As reported in numerous scientific research on the subject, these foods can help improve cholesterol levels, control weight, and reduce the risk of developing Alzheimer's disease, diabetes, and several types of cancer (Gantenbeinet al., 2021).

BRAIN FUNCTION IMPROVED

The Mediterranean diet may improve brain health and reduce the risk of Alzheimer's disease. Research has shown that healthy fats can help prevent cognitive decline and that there is a direct correlation between fish consumption and decreased prevalence of Alzheimer's. In 2018, the journal Neurology presented a two-year scientific study in which 70 brain scans were taken of individuals with no signs of dementia at the beginning of the study. At the end of the research, results showed that individuals who followed the Mediterranean diet had a smaller increase in deposits and a reduction in energy consumption-potential signs of Alzheimer's (Miranda et al., 2017).

REDUCED CANCER RISK

According to the results of a group study, diet is associated with a lower risk of stomach cancer (e.g., gastric adenocarcinoma).

References:
Davis C, Bryan J, Hodgson J, Murphy K. Definition of the Mediterranean Diet; a Literature Review. Nutrients. 2015 Nov 5;7(11):9139-53. doi: 10.3390/nu7115459.
Ekmekcioglu C. Nutrition and longevity - From mechanisms to uncertainties. Crit Rev Food Sci Nutr. 2020;60(18):3063-3082. doi: 10.1080/10408398.2019.1676698. Epub 2019 Oct 21.
Guasch-Ferré M, Willett WC. The Mediterranean diet and health: a comprehensive overview. J Intern Med. 2021 Sep;290(3):549-566. doi: 10.1111/joim.13333. Epub 2021 Aug 23.
Gantenbein KV, Kanaka-Gantenbein C. Mediterranean Diet as an Antioxidant: The Impact on Metabolic Health and Overall Wellbeing. Nutrients. 2021 Jun 6;13(6):1951. doi: 10.3390/nu13061951. PMID: 34204057; PMCID: PMC8227318.
Merra G, Noce A, Marrone G, Cintoni M, Tarsitano MG, Capacci A, De Lorenzo

A. Influence of Mediterranean Diet on Human Gut Microbiota. Nutrients. 2020 Dec 22;13(1):7. doi: 10.3390/nu13010007.

Mirabelli M, Chiefari E, Arcidiacono B, Corigliano DM, Brunetti FS, Maggisano V, Russo D, Foti DP, Brunetti A. Mediterranean Diet Nutrients to Turn the Tide against Insulin Resistance and Related Diseases. Nutrients. 2020 Apr 12;12(4):1066. doi: 10.3390/nu12041066.

Miranda A, Gómez-Gaete C, Mennickent S. Dieta mediterránea y sus efectos benéficos en la prevención de la enfermedad de Alzheimer [Role of Mediterranean diet on the prevention of Alzheimer disease]. Rev Med Chil. 2017 Apr;145(4):501-507. Spanish. doi: 10.4067/S0034-98872017000400010.

Sánchez-Villegas A, Martínez-González MA, Estruch R, Salas-Salvadó J, Corella D, Covas MI, Arós F, Romaguera D, Gómez-Gracia E, Lapetra J, Pintó X, Martínez JA, Lamuela-Raventós RM, Ros E, Gea A, Wärnberg J, Serra-Majem L. Mediterranean dietary pattern and depression: the PREDIMED randomized trial. BMC Med. 2013 Sep 20;11:208. doi: 10.1186/1741-7015-11-208.

FOCUS – THE MEDITERRANEAN DIET: AN EVERYDAY LIFESTYLE

Mediterranean communities take a holistic approach to life. Diet is only one slice of the big pie that is a lifestyle.

People have strong social ties, which improves physical and mental health. It has been shown that community involvement and regular visits to friends and family can increase longevity by up to 50 percent. As we discussed, this aspect helps keep depression and anxiety at bay and strengthens the immune system. Sitting down daily for a leisurely meal with the family and sipping a glass of red wine that relaxes the nerves can do wonders for the overall well-being.

Daily physical activity relieves stress accumulated during the day is a typical feature of the Mediterranean lifestyle. Instead of spending hours in traffic, people walk or bike to work. They walk along the road or by the sea. They buy fresh ingredients for their next meal, stopping to chat with friends they meet along the way.

People who live in these regions also know the benefits and sacredness of leisure time. They take more vacation time than the average American. They try to have lunch away from their desks, perhaps spent with family. It is an important part of their day. It is a way of managing stress that comes naturally to them.

CURIOSITIES: THE MEDITERRANEAN DIET ORIGINS

"Blue zones" is the term used to refer to geographic areas called "longevity hotspots," or regions where residents live longer and healthier lives. This research was conducted in the 1970s by National Geographic. In these blue zones, it was seen that the elderly are much more active and energetic than in the United States.

In particular, Ikaria in Greece, Oligastra (Sardinia) in It-aly, Okinawa in Japan, Nicoya in Costa Rica, and Loma Linda in California was studied.

Are you surprised to see America on the list? No surprise at all! This area is concentrated in the suburb of San Bernadino, which has avoided alcohol, cigarettes, tobacco, and often unconsumed drugs, focusing on a healthy diet and exercise similar to what we find in the Mediterranean.

These areas were identified because people living there have lower rates of chronic diseases and live well into old age. You may be curious to know why. Well, there are some similarities in the lifestyles of the people living in these communities:

- Legumes, such as lentils, beans, and chickpeas, form the basis of many meals
- Lots of vegetable consumption
- Nuts are a source of healthy fats
- Fish is consumed in blue zones that are close to the sea
- White meat is the major source of proteins
- Daily physical activity is part of everyday life
- They have a strong social network
- Sleep is a priority. People in Blue Zones get enough sleep at night and take afternoon naps.
- Calorie restriction is a usual way of life
- Spirituality is important
- Having a purpose in life
- The diet is rich in whole grains
- Periodic fasting is practiced
- Seniors are not separated from their families
- Alcohol is consumed in moderation

Two Blue Zones fall in the Mediterranean Sea – Sardinia and Ikaria. The same patterns are found in other communities living near the Mediterranean Sea. With decades of research to back it up, the Mediterranean Diet has become the gold standard for healthy eating. It promotes a healthy weight, keeps chronic diseases at bay, and helps people live longer.

FOOD GROUP	RECOMMENDED FOODS
Vegetables (Fiber)	Mushrooms, asparagus, squash, zucchini, Brussel sprouts, cauliflower, eggplant, spinach, kale, bell peppers, broccoli, onions
Nuts and seeds (Fat)	Macadamia nuts, walnuts, pumpkin seeds, almonds, sunflower seeds, cashews, hazelnuts
Fish (Protein)	Salmon, sardines, herring, tuna and mackerel
Beans and legumes (Protein)	Any beans, black-eyed peas, green beans, chickpeas, edamame, peas, lentils, miso, tofu
Fruits (Fiber and Sugars)	Berries, pineapple, pears, oranges, bananas, apples, melon, avocados, kiwi, dates
Whole grains and starchy vegetables (Carbohydrates)	Quinoa, sweet potato, oats, couscous, barley, whole grain bread, brown rice, whole grain pasta, red skin potato

WHAT TO LIMIT?

However, there are several things you should avoid when eating Mediterranean-style meals.

ALCOHOL CONSUMPTION

Red wine should be your alcoholic beverage if you follow the Mediterranean diet. This is because red wine has health benefits, especially for the heart. However, you should limit your alcohol consumption to one drink per day for women and men over the age of 60, and two drinks per day for men aged 60 and younger. One drink corresponds to five ounces of wine, twelve ounces of beer, or 1.5 ounces of 80-proof liquor.

HIGH SATURATED FAT

Butter should be avoided if you're following a Mediterranean diet. Instead, use olive oil, which has many heart health benefits and is lower in saturated fat than butter. Butter includes 7 grams of saturated fat per tbsp., while olive oil has about two grams, as per USDA National Nutrient Database.

REFINED GRAINS

Whole grains, including spelt, couscous, millet, and brown rice, are staples of the Mediterranean diet. If you're following this eating plan, you'll want to minimize your intake of refined grains such as white pasta and white bread.

PROCESSED MEAT

Processed meat (such as hot dogs or bacon) should be avoided or limited as much as possible. According to a study in the British Medical Journal, chronic consumption of red meat, especially processed types, is linked to an increased risk of mortality.

WEEK 1

DAYS	BREAKFAST	LUNCH	DINNER
Day 1	Special Figs Greek Yogurt	Cauliflower and Farro Salad	Autumn Chicken with Cabbage
Day 2	Avocado Salad with Fruit Yogurt	Winter Gnocchi Salad	Pan-Fried Swordfish
Day 3	Almond And Chia Porridge	Tuna and Couscous	Curried Cauliflower
Day 4	Mediterranean Toasted Tomato Baguette	Autumn Pumpkin Risotto	Tyrrhenian Sea Chicken Meatballs
Day 5	Breakfast Pizza	Halibut In Herb Crust	Potato And Bean Soup
Day 6	Quinoa Muffins	Bouillabaisse Soup	Mediterranean Marinated Grilled Chicken
Day 7	Mediterranean Millet	Lentil Soup	Shrimp Salad with Avocado

WEEK 2

DAYS	BREAKFAST	LUNCH	DINNER
Day 1	Salmon and Chard Crepes	White Bean Soup	Grilled Swordfish
Day 2	Vanilla Greek Yogurt with Honey	Chickpea and Pasta Soup	Italian-Style Turkey Patties in Green Sauce
Day 3	Raspberry Oats	Casserole of White Beans, Zucchini and Squash	Halibut Parcel with Olives and Capers
Day 4	Moroccan-Style Chickpea Fritters	Spicy Zucchini	Chicken Gyros Wrapped in Lettuce
Day 5	Shakshuka with Avocado	Beef Stew	Coconut Marinated Salmon
Day 6	Mediterranean Coast Avocado Toast	Vegetable Paella	Grilled Chicken with Oregano
Day 7	Almond and Chia Porridge	Veggie Cake	Mediterranean Coast-Style Grilled Octopus

		WEEK 3	
DAYS	**BREAKFAST**	**LUNCH**	**DINNER**
Day 1	Raspberry Oats	Winter Gnocchi Salad	Greek-Style Chicken and Barley
Day 2	Couscous with Dried Fruit	Minestrone Soup	Spicy Garlic Salmon
Day 3	Quinoa Muffins	Mediterranean-Style Sautéed Black Cabbage	Cacciatore Italian-Style Chicken
Day 4	Special Figs Greek Yogurt	Rice Soup with Chicken and Chard	Mediterranean-Style Squid Tubes
Day 5	Mediterranean-Style Blueberry Pancakes	Autumn Pumpkin Risotto	Chicken with Artichokes
Day 6	Salmon and Chard Crepes	Baked Mushrooms and Tomatoes	Halibut with Lemon and Basil
Day 7	Vanilla Greek Yogurt with Honey	Salmon Salad with Pecans	Greek Yogurt Chicken with Mint

		WEEK 4	
DAYS	**BREAKFAST**	**LUNCH**	**DINNER**
Day 1	Couscous with Dried Fruit	Salmon and Vegetable Soup	Baked Chicken Breast
Day 2	Shakshuka with Avocado	Chickpea and Pasta Soup	Halibut with Lemon and Basil
Day 3	Mediterranean Toasted Tomato Baguette	Halloumi	Mediterranean Chicken Skillet with Mushrooms
Day 4	Special Figs Greek Yogurt	Genovese Pesto Slices	Roast Beef and Asparagus Involtini
Day 5	Raspberry Oats	Pork and Bean Stew	Parmesan Salmon
Day 6	Mediterranean Coast Avocado Toast	Mint and Toasted Pita Salad	Special Margherita Pizza
Day 7	Mediterranean Millet	Mushroom and Chicken Soup	Shrimp Salad

	WEEK 5		
DAYS	**BREAKFAST**	**LUNCH**	**DINNER**
Day 1	Greek Yogurt with Honey	Phoenicians Bean Salad	Greek-style Stuffed Squid
Day 2	Blueberry Pancakes	Italian Minestrone Soup	Mediterranean Style Spicy Deviled Eggs
Day 3	Overnight Oatmeal with Figs	Calabrese Pasta	Italian style Chicken Meatballs
Day 4	Mediterranean Millet	Blue Zone Tuna Salad	Greek-style Potatoes
Day 5	Shakshuka in Crusty Bread	Carrot and Lentil Soup	Chicken Caprese Hasselback
Day 6	Mediterranean Avocado Toast	Crispy Veggie Pizza	Mediterranean Chicken Skillet with Mushrooms
Day 7	Pumpkin-flavored Quinoa	Couscous with Feta Cheese	Skimmed Chicken and Artichokes with Lemon

	WEEK 6		
DAYS	**BREAKFAST**	**LUNCH**	**DINNER**
Day 1	Caramelized Figs-sweetened Greek Yogurt	Chickpea Soup Pasta	Salmon Fillet with Sweet Chili Sauce
Day 2	Scrambled Egg Breakfast Bowl	Brussels Sprouts and Pistachios	Cashew Sauce Margherita Pizza
Day 3	Breakfast Couscous with Fruit	Tabouli Salad	Chicken Breast Tomato Bruschetta
Day 4	Chickpea Fritters	Grilled Fish Fillet with Genovese Pesto Sauce	Beef Stew
Day 5	Overnight Oatmeal with Figs	Boscaiola Gnocchi Salad	Mediterranean Turkey Meatballs
Day 6	Buckwheat Pancakes	Curried Chickpea Burgers	Chicken with Sicilian Olive
Day 7	Mediterranean Special Panini	Veggie Cake	Artichokes in Braised Chicken

WEEK 7

DAYS	BREAKFAST	LUNCH	DINNER
Day 1	Greek Yogurt with Honey	Grilled Vegetarian Panini	Shrimp Salad with Avocado
Day 2	Blueberry Pancakes	Vegetarian Tortilla Wraps	Tuscan Veggie Soup
Day 3	Mediterranean Millet	Carrot Cake Balls	Curry Crispy Chicken Meatballs
Day 4	Spinach and Egg Toast	Italian-style Grilled Octopus	White Bean Soup
Day 5	Italian Seasoned Omelet	Pasta Salad with Arugula and Asparagus	Mediterranean Turkey Meatballs
Day 6	Pumpkin-flavored Quinoa	Italian Style Cauliflower with Balsamic Raisins	Baked Cod with Tomatoes
Day 7	Breakfast Couscous with Fruit	Quinoa Salad with Veggies	Ground Turkey

WEEK 8

DAYS	BREAKFAST	LUNCH	DINNER
Day 1	Caramelized Figs-sweetened Greek Yogurt	Quinoa Salad with Veggies	Crab Patties
Day 2	Scrambled Egg Breakfast Bowl	Portuguese Style Salad	Crispy Veggie Pizza
Day 3	Greek Yogurt with Honey	Lentil Soup	Chicken and Dried Fruit Casserole
Day 4	Blueberry Pancakes	Healthy Tuna and Bean Rolls	Beef Stew Braised in Red Wine
Day 5	Overnight Oatmeal with Figs	Sicilian Pesto Gnocchi	Cacciatora-Tuscan Chicken
Day 6	Mediterranean Millet	Feta Spinach and Sweet Red Pepper Muffins	Sicilian-style Spaghetti with Tuna and Capers
Day 7	Buckwheat Pancakes	The Original Style Baked Bread	Greek Flavored Chicken Couscous

A healthy eating pattern for people includes healthy choices, favorite foods, dining out, and alcohol in moderation (if desired).

Are you confused about where to start? Or how to do grocery shopping and prepare your next meal? I will help you with some simple practice examples before following your 60-day meal plan.

What does a daily meal plan look like?

Here is a general guideline before you work with a registered nutritionist dietician:

NUTRIENTS	MEDITERRANEAN DIET	DIETARY GUIDELINES	
		Women	**Men**
		19-25y: 2200	19-25y: 2800
Calories	2152	26-50y: 2000	26-45y: 2600
		51+y: 1800	46-65y: 2400
			65+y: 2200
Carbohydrate (% of calories)	50%	45-65%	45-65%
Protein (% of calories)	30%	10-35%	10-35%
Total Fat (% of calories)	20%	20-35%	20-35%
Saturated Fat (% of calories)	8%	10%	10%
Cholesterol (mg)	300	no restriction warning to limit the daily intake	no restriction warning to limit the daily intake
Potassium (mg)	4,700	4,700	4,700
Sodium (mg)	2,300	2,300	2,300
Calcium (mg)	1,200	1,000	1,000
Vitamin A (mcg)	900	700	900
Vitamin C (mg)	90	75	90
Iron (mg)	18	18	8

What should your plate look like?

FOOD GROUP	SERVING	SERVING SIZE	TIP
Fruit	3-4 daily	1 medium-sized fruit 1 cup fresh cut cup dried	(At least) 1 serving of berries daily
Fish, egg, poultry (white meat)	2-3 times per week	3-4 ounces	For fish choose Omega 3s source
Vegetables	4-5 daily	½ cup cooked 1 cup raw	Try to eat: 1 cruciferous veg, 2 leafy greens, and 2 other vegetables daily
Beans and legumes	1-3 daily	1 cup fresh peas or sprouted lentils cup hummus or bean dip, ½ cup cooked,	Use in place of meat
Nuts and seeds	(At least) 3 per week	cup, 2 Tbsp seed butter or nuts	Use raw, unsalted, and dry roasted
Whole grains and starchy vegetables	3-6 daily	1 slice of bread ½ cup cooked 1 oz dry cereal	Try to have equal servings daily of starchy vegetables* and whole grains. "Whole" should be your first ingredient for bread and pasta
Red Meat	Monthly	3-4 ounces	Use fresh red meat (not processed)
Sweets	Monthly	3-4 ounces	Avoid bag sweets

*Examples of starchy vegetables include: Corn, Sweet potatoes, White potatoes, Green peas, Beets, Acorn squash, Butternut squash, Turnips, and Carrots.

Additional Helpful Tips:
- Avoid red meat. No more than 2 times per month.
- Avoid saturated fats (fried foods, cookies, cakes, etc.).
- 1 tbsp. ground flaxseed per day. Tip: Stir into a smoothie or oatmeal.
- Low to moderate in dairy products (mostly cheese and yogurt). Limit cheese to 3 portions weekly. Tip: opt for skim milk or 1% milk, yogurt, and cottage cheese. Eat plain, light, or partly skimmed cheese. Avoid greasy dairy products, cream, and cream-based sauces and dressings.
- Extra virgin olive oil is used as a common source of monounsaturated fat—1 tbsp. per day (maximum 4 tbsp. per day).
- Low to moderate use of eggs (zero to 4 times per week)
- Low to moderate wine (one glass of red wine per day) is normally consumed with meals. If you don't drink alcohol, there's no reason to start.

Snacks
There are many snack options available for the Mediterranean diet.
Suitable snacks include:

- Nuts (30g)
- Avocado on whole-grain toast (50g)
- Yogurt (120mL)
- Whole fruits (e.g., oranges, grapes, and plums) (100g)
- Dried fruits, including figs and apricots (30g)
- Hummus with carrots, celery, or other vegetables (50g)

Before you start, remember…

The Mediterranean diet is healthy eating at its best. It provides the ideal balance of unrefined carbohydrates, lean proteins, and healthy fats combined with nutrient-dense, fresh seasonal produce. Meals cooked according to the principles of the Mediterranean Diet are full of intense natural flavor.

These principles are at the base of this book's recipes so that you can cook great-tasting meals for your family and friends. Your food will not just taste delicious, but also will be rich in healthy ingredients, putting you on the way to good health and longevity.

BREAKFAST PIZZA

Prep	Portion	Cook
5 m	6	15 m

Per Serving

Calories: 384; Fat: 16g; Sat fat: 4.3 g; Carb: 47g; Protein: 14g

Ingredients:

- 1 x 12-inch thin pre-cooked pizza base
- 3/4 cup reduced-fat cottage cheese
- 1 tsp smoked sweet paprika (divided)
- 1 tsp garlic powder
- 1/2 cup sun-dried tomatoes (not packed in oil)
- 1 cup porcini mushrooms, sliced
- 3 cups chard, roughly chopped
- 2 tbsp extra virgin olive oil
- 2 tbsp balsamic vinegar
- 1/4 tsp white pepper, divided
- 1/4 tsp Sea salt salt
- 6 large free-range eggs

Directions:

1. Preheat the oven to 450°F, with the rack in the center.
2. Place the pizza base on a large baking sheet. Using a knife, spread the ricotta cheese over the base in an even layer. Sprinkle 1/2 tsp paprika over the cheese and 1 tsp garlic powder.
3. Top the topped cheese with sun-dried tomatoes and sliced mushrooms.
4. Place beets in a large bowl and sprinkle with oil, vinegar, and 1/8 tsp pepper and salt. With clean hands, toss and coat the chard with the dressing for a few minutes until softened and well coated.
5. Arrange the seasoned chard on top of the pizza. Create a nest in the chard for each egg. Gently break each egg into a nest and season with the remaining paprika, pepper, and salt.
6. Bake the pizza for 12 to 15 minutes until the egg white is no longer runny and the yellow is almost set, but not quite.
7. Cut into slices and serve hot.

Tip: Dried tomatoes should be softened before use if you are not using those in oil. Simply soak the tomatoes in boiling water until softened and drain before using.

Prep	**Portion**	**Cook**	**Per Serving**
10 m	1 Serving	15 m	Calories 296; Fat 16g; Sodium 394mg; Carb 21g; Fiber 7g; Sugar 5g; Protein 18g

SPINACH AND EGG TOAST

- 1 tbsp. extra-virgin olive oil
- 1 cup and a half of spinach
- 2 eggs, beaten
- 1 slice whole-wheat bread, toasted
- ½ cup raspberries, chopped
- Kosher salt and black pepper, to taste

Directions:

1. Heat the oil in a non-stick skillet over medium-high heat.
2. Add the spinach and cook for 5-7 minutes.
3. Add the eggs to the same skillet and cook for 5 minutes, stirring every 2 minutes.
4. Add salt and pepper to your taste.
5. Serve with toast and raspberries as a garnish and enjoy!

Substitution Tip: Substitute raspberries for your favorite berries or avocado.

Prep	**Portion**	**Cook**	**Per Serving**
10 m	4 Servings	5 m	Calories 253; Fat 11g; Sodium 107mg; Carb 34g; Fiber 9g; Sugar 6g; Protein 10g

CHICKPEA FRITTERS

1 cup water
1 cup of chickpea flour
½ tsp. salt
½ tsp. pepper
1 tsp. turmeric
1 tbsp. extra-virgin olive oil
3 spring onions, diced
1 red bell pepper, diced, optional
½ tsp. chili flakes, optional

Directions:

1. Add the water, flour, salt, pepper, chili flakes (optional), and turmeric to a blender. Blend and then set aside.
2. Heat the oil in a non-stick skillet.
3. Add the spring onions to the flour mixture.
4. Add one tbsp. of the mixture to the hot skillet and cook for 3 minutes.
5. Flip the fritters with a spatula and cook for another 2 minutes.
6. Serve warm. Garnish with green onions.

Substitution tip: For a milder taste, omit the chili flakes.

Prep	**Portion**	**Cook**	**Per Serving**
10 m	12 Makes	30 m	Calories: 135; Fat: 8g; Sat fat: 3.2 g; Carb: 7g; Protein: 8g

QUINOA MUFFINS

- 1 cup cooked quinoa
- 6 eggs, beaten
- Salt and black pepper to taste
- 1 cup grated Swiss cheese
- 1 small yellow onion, chopped
- 1 cup white mushrooms, sliced
- ½ cup sun-dried tomatoes, chopped

Directions:

1. Combine the eggs with salt, pepper, and the ingredients in a bowl and beat well.
2. Divide the mixture into a silicone muffin pan, bake at 350°F for 30 minutes and serve for breakfast.

Serving tip: Serve with yogurt.

Substitution tip: You can add more spices or toppings or play with different Substitutions of vegetables.

Prep
10 m

Portion
6 Servings

Cook
7 m

Per Serving
Calories: 359; Fat: 14g; Sat fat: 3.1g; Carb: 51g; Protein: 10g

SPECIAL FIGS GREEK YOGURT

- 8 ounces fresh figs, halved
- 3 tbsp. honey, divided
- 2 cups Greek yogurt
- Pinch of ground cinnamon
- ¼ cup pistachios, chopped

Directions:

1. In a preheated skillet over medium heat, add 1 tbsp. honey and cook for about 2 minutes.
2. In the skillet, place figs, cut sides down, and cook for about 5 minutes or until caramelized.
3. Remove from heat and set aside for about 2-3 minutes.
4. Divide yogurt among serving bowls and top each with caramelized fig halves.
5. Sprinkle with pistachios and cinnamon.
6. Drizzle each bowl with the remaining honey and serve.

Serving tip: Serve with blueberries on top.

Suggestion Tip: You can use orange zest to add flavor.

Prep
1 m

Portion
6 Servings

Cook
0 m

Per Serving
Calories: 336; Fat: 16g; Sat fat: 2.7g; Carb: 51g; Protein: 5g

AVOCADO SALAD WITH FRUIT YOGURT

- 3 medium-sized ripe avocados, peeled and diced
- 2 tbsp lemon juice (plus 1 tsp)
- 1 tbsp finely grated lemon zest
- 2 tbsp raw honey
- 1/2 cup Greek yogurt
- 1 medium-sized firm banana, cut into slices
- 1 kg canned mandarin oranges, drained
- 1 cup seedless grapes, cut in half
- 1 granny smith apple, cut in pieces

Directions:

1. Place diced avocados in a bowl with 2 tbsp lemon juice and toss to coat.
2. Whisk together the remaining lemon juice, lemon zest, honey, and yogurt in a separate bowl.
3. Add the banana, mandarin oranges, grapes, and apple to the bowl with the avocado and mix gently.
4. Distribute the salad in the bowls and serve with the yogurt.

Prep
10 m

Portion
4 Servings

Cook
20 m

Per Serving
Calories: 207; Fat: 8g; Sat fat: 0.6g; Carb: 30g; Protein: 5g

ALMOND AND CHIA PORRIDGE

- 15 ounces blueberries
- 3 cups organic almond milk
- ⅓ cup chia seeds, dried
- 1 tsp of vanilla extract
- 1 tbsp of honey
- ¼ tsp ground cardamom

Directions:

1. Pour the almond milk into a saucepan and bring it to a boil.
2. Remove from the heat and cool the almond milk to room temperature for 15 minutes.
3. Add the vanilla extract, honey, and ground cardamom. Stir well.
4. Add the chia seeds and stir again.
5. Close the lid and let the chia seeds soak in the liquid for 20-25 minutes.
6. Transfer the cooked oatmeal to serving ramekins.

Serving tip: Serve with fresh raspberries.

Recipe tip: Stir the chia seeds well to prevent lumps from forming.

	Prep 5 m	**Portion** 4 Servings	**Cook** 8 m	**Per Serving** Calories: 335; Fat: 7g; Sat fat: 1 g; Carb: 55g; Protein: 15g

MEDITERRANEAN TOASTED TOMATO BAGUETTE

- 2 baguettes, cut in half lengthwise
- 4 tbsp crushed garlic
- 2 ripe variety tomatoes, grated
- 2 tbsp extra virgin olive oil
- 4 thin slices of smoked ham
- Freshly ground black pepper
- 1 tbsp flaked sea salt

Directions:

1. Preheat the oven to 500°F, with the rack in the center.
2. Place baguette halves on a baking sheet with open sides up and toast in the oven for 6 to 8 minutes, or until golden brown and crisp.
3. When the baguettes are well toasted, spread 1 tsp of crushed garlic on the face of each baguette. Top the garlic with the grated tomato. Spread the tomato in an even layer using a butter knife.
4. Drizzle the tomatoes with a small amount of olive oil. Add a slice of ham to each baguette and season to taste with black pepper before salting each baguette. Use about 1/4 tsp of salt for each baguette.

Plate the toasted baguettes and serve immediately.

Prep 10 m	**Portion** 8 Servings	**Cook** 15 m	**Per Serving** Calories: 249; Fat: 6g; Sat fat: 2.4 g; Carb: 41g; Protein: 8g

MEDITERRANEAN MILLET

- 2 cups millet
- 1 cup almond milk, unsweetened
- 1 cup water
- 1 cup coconut milk, unsweetened
- 1 tsp. ground cinnamon
- ½ tsp. ground ginger
- ¼ tsp. salt
- 1 tbsp. chia seeds
- 1 tbsp. cashew butter
- 4 ounces shredded coconut

Directions:

1. Combine coconut milk, almond milk, and water in a saucepan over medium heat; stir gently.
2. Add millet, stir well, and close lid.
3. Cook millet for 5 minutes.
4. Add the cinnamon, ground ginger, salt, and chia seeds. Stir well and continue to cook over medium heat for another 5 minutes.
5. Add the cashew butter and cook for another 5 minutes.
6. Remove the mixture from the heat and transfer it to serving bowls.
7. Sprinkle on the coconut. Serve and enjoy.

Substitution Tip: Substitute cashew butter for any nut butter.

Prep 15 m	**Portion** 4 Servings	**Cook** 13 m	**Per Serving** Calories: 262; Fat: 6g; Sat fat: 3.2 g; Carb: 45g; Protein: 11g

COUSCOUS WITH DRIED FRUIT

- 1 cup uncooked whole-wheat couscous
- 3 cups of low-fat milk
- ¼ cup dried currants
- 6 tsp dark brown sugar, divided
- Salt, to taste
- ⅓ cup dried apricots, chopped
- ¼ tsp of ground cinnamon
- 2 tsp unsalted butter, melted

Directions:

1. In a saucepan set over medium-high heat, add the milk and cook for about 3 minutes or until completely heated.
2. Remove from heat and immediately stir in couscous, 4 tsp brown sugar, dried fruit, salt, and cinnamon.
3. Cover the saucepan and set aside for about 10 minutes.
4. Divide the couscous mixture evenly among four bowls.
5. Top each with the remaining brown sugar and melted butter evenly.
6. Serve immediately.

Serving tip: Serve with a few toasted almonds on top.

Substitution tip: Nutmeg can also be added.

Prep

3 m

Portion

2 Servings

Cook

15 m

Per Serving

Calories: 384; Fat: 22g; Sat fat: 5.6 g; Carb: 39g; Protein: 12g

SALMON AND CHARD CREPES

- 1 cup chopped fresh beets
- 1 tbsp of flax meal
- 1 tbsp nutritional yeast
- 1/4 tsp chopped dried thyme
- 1 small bunch of fresh parsley, chopped
- ½ tsp. Sea salt
- Freshly ground black pepper
- 2 large free-range eggs
- 2 tbsp extra virgin olive oil
- 3 oz. smoked wild salmon
- 1/2 large Hass avocado, sliced
- 2 tbsp. feta cheese, crumbled
- 1 tbsp fresh lemon juice

Directions:

1. Combine the beets, flax meal, nutritional yeast, thyme, and parsley in a blender. Add a pinch of salt and pepper, or more to taste, before blending the mixture until the chard is thin. Add the eggs and blend until the mixture has just come together.

2. In a large skillet over medium heat, heat 1 tsp of olive oil. When the oil is hot, add half of the beet mixture and gently move the pan until the mixture is evenly distributed on the bottom—Fry for about 3 minutes, or until the crepe is no longer bulging but not completely firm.

3. Top the crepe with half the salmon, avocado, and feta. Drizzle the entire crepe with 1 tsp of lemon juice while still in the pan. Carefully transfer the crepe to a plate and keep it warm while you repeat the process with the remaining ingredients.

4. Serve the crepes warm and enjoy.

Prep

2 m

Portion

2 Servings

Cook

0 m

Per Serving

Calories 270; Fat 8 g; Sat Fat: 5.2g; Carb 41g; Protein: 9g

VANILLA GREEK YOGURT WITH HONEY

- 1/3 tsp. vanilla essence
- 2 cups Greek yogurt
- 1/4 - 1/2 tsp. honey
- 1/3 tsp. ground nutmeg
- 1 cup blueberries

Directions:

1. Whisk together the vanilla and yogurt in a medium-sized glass bowl. Gradually stir in a small amount of honey, tasting for sweetness as you go, and add honey to taste, but not exceeding 1/2 cup. Once the yogurt is sweetened to your liking, whisk in the nutmeg.

2. Scrape yogurt into serving bowls, and garnish with blueberries before serving.

Substitution Tip: You can use low-fat yogurt or cottage cheese and a pinch of brown sugar.

Per Serving

Calories: 427; Total fat: 21g; Saturated fat: 5g; Carb: 39g; Protein: 23g; Sodium: 674mg; Fiber: 7g

Prep

5 m

Makes

4 Servings

Cook

0 m

MEDITERRANEAN SPECIAL PANINI

- 1 sandwich (12oz.)
- 2 tbsp. extra virgin olive oil
- 8 large eggs, hard-boiled and cut into rounds
- 1/2 cup black olives, pitted and cut in half
- 2 cherry tomatoes, cut into thin rounds
- 12 fresh basil leaves

Directions:

1. Cut the sandwich in half horizontally and spread the inside of each slice with 1 tbsp. of olive oil.

2. Begin building the sandwich by placing a single layer of hard-boiled egg slices on one half of the sandwich, followed by olives, sliced tomatoes, and finally, the basil leaves.

3. Place the remaining sandwich slice on top. Slice the sandwich and serve.

Ingredient tip: Use milk bread to add more taste.

Prep
10 m

Portion
2 Servings

Cook
0 m

Per Serving

Calories 348; Fat 20.8g; Sodium 249mg; Carb 38.7g; Fiber 12.3g; Sugar 37.4g; Protein 7.1g

MEDITERRANEAN AVOCADO TOAST

- *1 tbsp. goat cheese, crumbled*
- *1 avocado, peeled, pitted, and mashed*
- *A pinch of sea salt and black pepper*
- *2 slices whole-wheat bread, toasted*
- *½ tsp. Lime juice*
- *1 persimmon, thinly sliced*
- *1 fennel bulb, thinly sliced*
- *2 tsp. Honey*
- *2 tbsp. pomegranate seeds*

Directions

1. *Combine avocado pulp with salt, pepper, lime juice, and cheese and whisk in a bowl.*

2. *Spread this mixture on toasted bread slices, top each slice with the remaining ingredients and serve for breakfast.*

Ingredient Tip: Choose perfectly ripe avocados; unripe avocados become challenging to mash and are not flavorful.

Substitution Tip: Serve with scrambled eggs.

Prep
5 m

Portion
4 Servings

Cook
15 m

Per Serving

Calories: 336; Total fat: 8g; Saturated fat: 5g; Carb: 54g; Protein: 12g; Sodium: 266mg; Fiber: 3g

BREAKFAST COUSCOUS WITH FRUIT

- *1 cinnamon stick*
- *3 cups milk*
- *1/4 tsp. Sea salt*
- *2 tbsp. honey (extra for serving)*
- *1/4 cup dried raisins*
- *1/2 cup dried apricots, chopped*
- *1 cup uncooked whole-wheat couscous*
- *4 tbsp. melted butter*

Directions

1. *Place the cinnamon stick, along with the milk, in a medium-sized saucepan over medium-high heat, and heat until just under a simmer. The milk should simmer gently but not boil.*

2. *Transfer the pot to a wooden cutting board and gently whisk in the salt, honey, raisins, apricots, and couscous.*

3. *Place a lid on the pot and allow the mixture to stand for about 12 minutes or until the couscous has softened.*

4. *Divide the couscous among four bowls, and serve topped with 1 tsp. butter per bowl and extra honey if desired.*

Prep
10 m

Portion
6 Servings

Cook
15 m

Per Serving

Calories 301; Fat 13.9g; Sodium 140mg; Carb 16g; Fiber 1.4g; Sugar 36.8g; Protein 3g

BLUEBERRY PANCAKES

- *15 ounces blueberries*
- *¼ tsp. Sea salt*
- *3 tbsp. olive oil*
- *3 eggs*
- *1 tsp. vanilla extract*
- *⅔ cup sugar*
- *1 cup milk*
- *½ tsp. baking powder*
- *1½ cups unbleached whole wheat flour*

Directions:

1. *Mix flour, baking powder, sugar, and salt in a bowl.*

2. *In another bowl, beat the eggs and milk.*

3. *Add the egg and milk mixture to the flour mixture. Stir and add the blueberries. Set the mixture aside for 1 hour.*

4. *Heat a skillet over medium-high heat.*

5. *Pour enough batter onto the pan for one pancake. Cook on both sides.*

6. *Repeat until all the batter is used.*

7. *Top with some blueberries.*

Substitution tip: Use aluminum-free baking powder for the best taste.

Prep	Portion	Cook	Per Serving
5 m	4 Servings	15-20 m	Calories: 246; Fat: 20g; Sat fat: 5.11 g; Carb: 10g; Protein: 7g

SHAKSHUKA WITH AVOCADO

- 4 tbsp extra virgin olive oil (divided)
- 1 small zucchini, cut into small pieces
- 1 small green bell pepper, cut into slices
- 1 tsp crushed garlic
- 1/2 small shallot, chopped
- 1/2 tsp smoked sweet paprika
- 1/4 tsp ground coriander seeds
- 1/2 tsp ground turmeric
- 1/2 tsp ground cumin
- 1/2 cup canned tomatoes, whole or chopped
- 3.5 ounces fresh beets, coarsely chopped
- 4 large free-range eggs
- 1/4 cup goat cheese, grated
- 1 small Hass avocado, sliced
- 2 tbsp fresh lemon juice

Directions:

1. Preheat the oven to 425°F, with the rack in the center.

2. In a large, oven-safe skillet, heat 2 tbsp olive oil over medium heat. When the oil is hot, sauté the zucchini, peppers, garlic, and scallions for about 3 to 4 minutes, or until the scallions are translucent and the vegetables have softened. Stir in the paprika, coriander seeds, turmeric, and cumin for 30 seconds, so the fragrances blend. Add the tomatoes and chard to the skillet, and stir-fry for about 1 minute, or until the chard has reduced.

3. Remove the skillet from the heat. Using a wooden spoon or ladle, create pockets in the shakshuka. Gently break each egg into its pocket, careful not to damage the yolks. Bake for 5 to 8 minutes until the egg whites are no longer runny, but the yellow is still firm.

Transfer the pan to a wooden cutting board and top the shakshuka with the goat cheese and avocado slices. Drizzle with the remaining olive oil and lemon juice. Serve warm and enjoy.

Prep	Portion	Cook	Per Serving
10 m	6 Serving	20 m	Calories 216; Fat 12.8g; Sodium 381mg; Carb 16.6g; Fiber 4.4g; Sugar 6.5g; Protein 11.2g

SHAKSHUKA IN CRUSTY BREAD

- 1 tsp. ground cumin
- 2 tbsp. extra-virgin olive oil
- 1 red bell pepper, chopped
- 6 eggs
- ¼ tsp. salt
- 3 garlic cloves, minced
- Ground black pepper, to taste
- 2 tbsp. tomato paste
- ½ tsp. smoked paprika
- 1 yellow onion, chopped
- ¼ tsp. red pepper flakes, plus more for garnish
- 2 tbsp. cilantro, chopped, for garnish
- ½ cup feta cheese, crumbled, for garnish
- 28 ounces roasted tomatoes, crushed
- Crusty bread, to serve

Directions:

1. Preheat oven to 375°F.

2. Heat the oil in a skillet over medium heat. Add and cook the bell pepper, onions, and salt for six minutes, stirring the mixture constantly.

3. Add the tomato paste, red pepper flakes, cumin, garlic, and paprika—Cook for an additional two minutes.

4. Add the crushed tomatoes and cilantro to the onion mixture. Allow simmering.

5. Reduce heat and simmer for five minutes.

6. Use salt and pepper to adjust the flavor.

7. Crack eggs into small wells made in different pan areas using a spoon.

8. Pour tomato mixture over eggs to help them cook while remaining intact.

9. Bake the skillet in the preheated oven for 12 minutes.

10. Garnish with cilantro, red pepper flakes, and feta cheese and serve.

Tip: Serve with crusty bread.

Cooking Tip: Adjust the timing to cook the eggs as you like.

Prep
5 m

Portion
1 Servings

Cook
5 m

Per Serving

Calories 325; Fat 25.2g; Sodium 992mg; Carb 9.4g; Fiber 2.1g; Sugar 5.4g; Protein 17.4g

SCRAMBLED EGG BREAKFAST BOWL

- 2 eggs
- 1 tsp. of extra-virgin olive oil
- ½ bell pepper, chopped
- ½ shallot, chopped
- ¼ cup feta cheese, crumbled
- ¼ cup olives pitted
- pepper
- Sea Salt

Direction:

1. In a bowl, beat the eggs with pepper and salt. Add the olives, shallots, bell pepper and cheese and mix well.
2. Heat the oil in a skillet over medium-high heat.
3. Add the egg mixture to the skillet and let it cook for 2 minutes, then begin scrambling the egg mixture.
4. Stir for an additional 3 minutes.

Tip: Garnish with parsley and serve.

Substitution tip: You can use goat cheese instead of feta.

Prep
5 m

Portion
4 Serving

Cook
30 m

Per Serving

Calories: 361; Total fat: 10g; Saturated fat: 1g; Carb: 65g; Protein: 9g; Sodium: 155mg;

PUMPKIN-FLAVORED QUINOA

- 1/2 cup quinoa, rinsed
- 3/4 cup steel-cut oats
- 1/4 tsp. sea salt
- 3 cups water
- 3 tbsp. honey
- 1 tsp. pumpkin pie spice
- 3/4 cup canned pumpkin
- 1/3 cup lightly toasted walnuts, coarsely chopped
- 1/2 cup dried blueberries
- Almond Milk

Directions:

1. Bring quinoa, oats, salt, and water to a boil in a medium saucepan over medium heat. Once the mixture is boiling, lower the heat, and simmer with the lid on the pot for 20 minutes, occasionally stirring to avoid burning.
2. Gently stir in the honey, pumpkin spice, and canned pumpkin. Transfer the pot to a wooden cutting board and let stand with the lid on the pot for about 10 minutes, or until all the liquid is absorbed and the quinoa and oats have softened.
3. Gently stir in the nuts and dried blueberries. Serve with a few splashes of almond milk, if desired.

Substitution Tip: You can use raspberry instead of blueberries.

Prep
10 m

Portion
2 Servings

Cook
1 night

Per Serving

Calories: 298; Fat: 7.8g; Sat fat: 0.9g; Carb: 51.1g; Fiber: 7.6g; Sugar: 27.6g; Protein: 9.5g

OVERNIGHT OATMEAL WITH FIGS

- 2 tbsp. almonds, chopped
- ½ cup quick oats
- 1 tbsp. chia seeds
- 1 tbsp. honey
- 1 cup unsweetened soy milk
- 2-3 fresh figs, sliced

Directions:

1. In a large bowl, mix oats, soy milk, almonds, and chia seeds until well combined.
2. Cover the bowl and refrigerate overnight.
3. Divide oatmeal evenly among serving bowls and drizzle with honey.
4. Serve with the fig slice topping.

Substitution tip: Almond milk can be used instead of soy milk.

Serving tip: Serve with a topping of crushed walnuts.

Prep	Portion	Cook	Per Serving
5 m	Servings	15-20 m	Calories: 204g; Total fat: 12g; Saturated fat: 4g; Carb: 13g; Protein: 11g; Fiber: 1g

ITALIAN SEASONED OMELET

- 1 tbsp. extra-virgin olive oil.
- 1/4 cup shallots, thinly sliced
- 1 large gold potato, thinly sliced
- 1/8 tsp. white pepper
- 1/8 tsp. cayenne pepper
- 1/4 tsp. Sea salt
- 1/4 tsp. dried thyme, crushed
- 1/4 tsp. dried rosemary, crushed
- 6 large eggs
- 2 tbsp. grated mozzarella cheese

Directions:

1. Set the oven rack to preheat on high, with the rack in the center of the oven.

2. In a large, oven-safe skillet, heat the oil before adding the scallions and fry for 2-3 minutes or until the scallions have softened. Use a slotted spoon to transfer the cooked scallions to a separate plate and tent to keep warm. Arrange the potato slices on the bottom of the pan in a single layer.

3. Add the pepper, cayenne pepper, salt, thyme, rosemary, and eggs to the bowl of scallions. Lightly whisk until the eggs are light and fluffy. Pour the egg mixture over the potatoes. Cover the pan with foil, and bake for 4-6 minutes, or until the eggs are no longer runny but not completely set.

4. Remove the pan from the oven and discard the foil. Sprinkle the cheese on top of the omelet before returning the pan to the oven and grill for 2-5 minutes. The cheese should be lightly toasted and the eggs completely set.

5. Allow the omelet to rest for about 5 minutes out of the oven before cutting and serving.

Substitution Tip: You can use Emmental cheese instead of mozzarella cheese.

Prep	Portion	Cook	Per Serving
10 m	4 Servings	10 m	Calories 196.4; Fat 5.8g; Sodium 269mg; Carb 25.7g; Fiber 6g; Sugar 5.2g; Protein 9.1g

BUCKWHEAT PANCAKES

- ¼ tsp. vanilla extract
- 1 cup buckwheat flour
- 1¼ tsp. baking powder
- ½ tsp. sugar
- ¼ tsp. salt
- 1¼ cup buttermilk
- 1 egg
- 1 tbsp. extra-virgin olive oil

Directions:

1. Whisk wet ingredients in one bowl and dry ingredients in another.

2. Mix the contents of both bowls.

3. Heat the olive oil in a skillet over medium heat.

4. Pour batter into batches and cook on both sides for about five minutes.

5. Top with a little honey and fresh berries.

Ingredient Tip: You can use almond or peanut butter for more protein.

Prep	Portion	Cook	Per Serving
10 m	1 Servings	5 m	Calories: 356; Fat: 8g; Sat fat: 0.7 g; Carb: 77g; Protein: 9g

RASPBERRY OATS

- ½ cup fresh raspberries
- ¼ tsp vanilla
- ¾ cup unsweetened almond milk
- 1 tsp honey
- 2 tsp chia seeds
- ⅓ cup of oats
- A pinch of salt

Directions:

1. Add the raspberries to the bowl and mash them with a fork.

2. Transfer the raspberry puree and other ingredients to the glass jar and mix everything well.

3. Cover the jar with the lid and refrigerate overnight.

Serving tip: Add a drizzle of milk and serve.

Tip: Add two drops of almond extract.

Sides & Salads

ITALIAN STYLE CAULIFLOWER WITH BALSAMIC RAISINS

 Prep
10 m

 Portion
4

 Cook
55 m

 Per Serving

*Calories: 366; Total fat: 24g; Saturated fat: 3g; Carb: 37g;
Protein: 9g; Sodium: 1,102mg; Fiber: 7g*

Ingredients:

- 2 lb. cauliflower florets
- 6 tbsp. extra virgin olive oil (divided)
- 1 tsp. Kosher salt
- 1/2 tsp. freshly ground black pepper
- 3 tbsp. crushed garlic
- 2 tbsp. salted capers, rinsed and dried
- 3/4 cup fresh whole-wheat breadcrumbs
- 1 tbsp. anchovy paste
- 1/2 cup chicken broth
- 1 tbsp. balsamic vinegar
- 1/3 cup golden raisins
- 1 tbsp. fresh parsley, chopped

Directions:

1. Set the oven to preheat to 425°F, with the rack in the center of the oven.

2. Place cauliflower florets, 3 tbsp. oil, salt, and pepper in a large bowl. Stir until all florets are evenly coated. Place coated florets on a clean baking sheet and bake for about 45 minutes, turning every few minutes, or until florets are tender and nicely browned.

3. Meanwhile, heat the remaining olive oil in a large skillet over medium-low heat. When the oil is nice and hot, fry the garlic for about 5 minutes. Add the capers and fry for another 3 minutes. Add the breadcrumbs and fry for a few more minutes, stirring, until the crumbs are nicely toasted. Use a slotted spoon to scoop the fried bread crumbs into a clean bowl.

4. Raise the heat to medium-high, and whisk the anchovy paste and chicken broth in the same pan used to fry the bread crumbs. Whisk in the balsamic vinegar and raisins when the broth begins to boil. Continue to cook for another 5 minutes, or until the broth has reduced and the raisins have swelled.

5. Place the cooked cauliflower florets in a large bowl and mix them with the bread crumbs and raisins. Transfer the mixture to a serving dish and garnish with the parsley before serving.

	Prep	Portion	Cook	Per Serving
	10 m	2	0 m	Calories: 128 calories; Fat: 10.6 g; Sat. Fat: 1.7 g; Carb: 5.1 g; Protein: 1.1 g; Fiber: 1.3 g

FRESH TOMATO SALAD

- 2 medium tomatoes, cut into wedges
- ½ of a small red onion, peeled and sliced
- ½ tsp. minced garlic
- ¼ cup chopped fresh parsley
- ¼ cup chopped dill, fresh
- ¼ tsp. salt
- ¼ tsp. ground black pepper
- ¼ tsp. ground sumac
- 1 tbsp. extra-virgin olive oil
- 1 tsp. lemon juice
- ½ tsp. white wine vinegar

Directions

1. Take a large bowl, add the tomatoes, onion, parsley, dill, and garlic, and stir until mixed.
2. Then add the salt, black pepper, sumac, lemon juice, vinegar, and oil and toss until well combined.
3. Divide the salad between two bowls and serve.

Prep	Portion	Cook	Per Serving
10 m	4	20 m	Calories: 204; Total fat: 12g; Saturated fat: 2g; Carb: 21g; Protein: 5g; Sodium: 425mg; Fiber: 3g

BOSCAIOLA GNOCCHI SALAD

- 2 tbsp. extra virgin olive oil (plus 1/3 cup)
- 16 oz. potato gnocchi
- 1/2 lb. mushrooms, sliced
- 3 tbsp. freshly squeezed lemon juice
- 1/4 tsp. freshly ground black pepper
- 1/2 tsp. Sea salt
- 2 tbsp. lemon zest, finely grated
- 2 tbsp. capers, drained and chopped
- 1/3 cup fresh parsley, chopped
- 1/2 cup Kalamata olives, pitted and cut in half
- 5 ounces fresh chard, chopped
- 15 ounces canned chickpeas, drained and rinsed
- 3 large plum tomatoes, seeded and chopped
- 1/4 cup lightly toasted walnuts, chopped
- 1/2 cup feta cheese, crumbled

Directions:

1. Heat 1 tbsp. oil in a large skillet over medium-high heat. When the oil is nice and hot, fry the gnocchi for 6-8 minutes, or until golden brown. Scrape the cooked gnocchi into a large bowl and set aside.
2. Add 1 tbsp. of oil to the same skillet and heat. When the oil is nice and hot, fry the mushrooms for about 8 minutes until they turn a dark color and release their juices. Scrape the cooked mushrooms into the bowl with the gnocchi.
3. Pour 1/3 cup oil and 3 tbsp. lemon juice into the bowl, and stir gently to combine.
4. Add the pepper, salt, lemon zest, capers, parsley, olives, Swiss chard, chickpeas, and tomatoes to the bowl, stirring gently to combine.
5. Sprinkle the gnocchi with the walnuts and cheese and serve immediately.

Ingredient Tip: You can replace feta cheese with goat cheese.

Prep	Portion	Cook	Per Serving
10 m	8	0 m	Calories 157; Fat 12g;;Carb 2.3g; Fiber 0.3g; Sugar 0.7g; Protein 10g

MEDITERRANEAN STYLE SPICY DEVILED EGGS

- 8 eggs, hard-boiled
- 3 tbsp. Romano cheese, grated
- 1 tsp. of paprika
- 2 tbsp. of pesto
- 1 tbsp. of mayonnaise
- 1 tsp. mustard
- ½ tsp. ground black pepper
- 1 tbsp. dill
- 1 tsp. lime juice

Directions:

1. Peel the eggs and cut them in half.
2. Remove the yolks from the eggs and mash them thoroughly in a separate bowl with a fork.
3. Add the mustard, mayo, pesto, and lime juice. Blend the mixture with a hand blender.
4. Season the smooth mixture with ground black pepper and paprika.
5. Add the dill and Romano cheese to the egg yolk mixture and mix thoroughly with a fork.
6. Fill a pastry bag with the egg yolk mixture and fill the egg whites with it.
7. Place the cooked eggs in the refrigerator and chill until ready to serve.
8. Garnish with chopped green onions.

Substitution tip: Replace lime juice with lemon juice.

Prep	Portion	Cook	Per Serving
10 m	4	5-8 m	Calories 335; Fat 8 g; Sat Fat: 3.1g; Carb 18g; Protein: 45g

SQUID SALAD WITH BALSAMIC VINEGAR

- 1/4 cup balsamic vinegar
- 1 tsp raw honey
- 1 kg thawed and dried squid
- ½ tsp. extra virgin olive oil
- Pinch of cayenne pepper
- ¼ tsp. Kosher salt
- 1 tsp crushed garlic
- 2 tbsp freshly squeezed lemon juice
- 1 small zucchini, thinly sliced
- 8 cups arugula
- 2 oz. parmesan cheese, finely grated
- 8 sun-dried tomatoes in oil
- Freshly ground black pepper

Directions:

1. In a small saucepan over medium heat, bring the balsamic vinegar to a gentle simmer. Simmer the vinegar for about 4 minutes, or until half of it has evaporated. Transfer the saucepan to a wooden cutting board and gently add the honey with a whisk.

2. Prepare the squid by slicing each tentacle into rings of about 6 inches, taking special care to cut the largest tentacles in the center. This will prevent the squid from cooking unevenly.

3. In a large skillet over medium-high heat, heat the olive oil before adding the squid, cayenne pepper, 1/4 tsp salt, and crushed garlic. Fry the squid rings for about 4 minutes, or until all the rings are completely solid. Using tongs, transfer the cooked squid to a separate bowl and keep warm.

4. With the skillet still over medium-high heat, stir the sauce for about 3 minutes until it is thick enough to coat the back of a tsp. Spread the thickened sauce over the squid and drizzle with the lemon juice.

5. Arrange the zucchini slices on a serving plate and drizzle with 1 tbsp olive oil and 1/8 tsp salt. Spread the arugula over the zucchini slices and drizzle with the balsamic reduction. Add the parmesan cheese in an even layer. Decorate the outer edges of the plate with sun-dried tomatoes.

6. Arrange the cooked squid in the center of the salad plate and garnish with freshly ground black pepper before serving.

Prep	Portion	Cook	Per Serving
20 m	2	0 m	Calories: 190 calories; Fat: 10 g; Sat. Fat: g; Carb: 25.5 g; Protein: 3.2 g; Fiber: 3.1 g

TABOULI SALAD

- 2 tbsp. bulgur wheat, soaked, drained
- 2 small tomatoes, chopped
- 5 mint leaves, chopped
- 4 tbsp. chopped cucumber
- 4 tbsp. fresh parsley, chopped
- 1 large green onion, chopped
- ¼ tsp. salt
- 1 tbsp. extra-virgin olive oil
- 1 tbsp. lemon juice

Directions

1. Take a large bowl, place the tomato, cucumber, parsley, green onion, mint, bulgur wheat, and salt, and gently stir until combined.

2. Then add the oil and lemon juice, stir until well combined, and cover the bowl with its lid.

3. Place the bowl in the refrigerator and let it sit for 15 minutes.

4. Divide the salad between two bowls and then serve.

Prep	Portion	Cook	Per Serving
5 m	4	0 m	Calories 183; Fat 12 g; Sat Fat: 1.6 g; Carb 17g; Protein: 4g

MINT AND TOASTED PITA SALAD

- 1/4 tsp freshly ground black pepper
- 1/2 tsp ground sumac (extra for garnish)
- 1/2 tsp Kosher salt
- 1 tsp crushed garlic
- 1/2 cup extra virgin olive oil
- 1/2 cup freshly squeezed lemon juice
- 2 whole-wheat pita bread rolls, toasted and cut into bite-sized pieces
- 1 bunch of spring onions, thinly sliced
- 1 small green bell pepper, diced
- 1/4 cup fresh mint leaves, chopped
- 1/2 cup fresh parsley, chopped
- 2 heirloom tomatoes, diced
- 2 small English cucumbers, diced
- 2 cups romaine lettuce, shredded

Directions:

1. Whisk together the pepper, sumac, salt, garlic, olive oil, and lemon juice in a small glass bowl. Set aside.

2. Bring together the toasted pita bites, spring onions, bell peppers, mint, parsley, tomatoes, cucumbers, and shredded lettuce in a large bowl. Drizzle with olive oil dressing and serve immediately, garnishing with extra ground sumac.

Prep	Portion	Cook
20 m	8	20 m

Per Serving

Calories: 304; Fat: 16.9g; Sat fat: 3g; Carb: 31.3g; Fiber: 2.7g; Sugar: 3.2g; Protein: 8.3g

QUINOA SALAD WITH VEGGIES

- 1½ cups dry quinoa, rinsed and drained
- Salt and black pepper, to taste
- 1 tbsp. balsamic vinegar
- ½ tsp. dried thyme, crushed
- 1 (15-ounce) can low-sodium chickpeas, rinsed and drained
- ⅓ cup roasted red bell pepper, drained and sliced
- ¼ cup fresh basil, thinly sliced
- 3 cups water
- ½ cup extra virgin olive oil
- 2 small cloves of garlic, crushed
- ½ tsp. dried basil, crushed
- 3 cups fresh arugula
- ⅓ cup fresh Kalamata olives, pitted and sliced
- ⅓ cup feta cheese, crumbled

Directions:

1. Fill a saucepan with water and add ½ tsp. salt and the quinoa. Bring to a boil over high heat.
2. Reduce heat, cover, and cook for about 20 minutes or until all liquid is absorbed.
3. Remove from heat, and with a fork, fluff the quinoa.
4. Set aside to cool completely.
5. For the dressing: In a bowl, mix the olive oil with the garlic, vinegar, dried herbs, salt, and black pepper until well combined.
6. Mix the chickpeas, quinoa, arugula, bell pepper, olives, and feta cheese in a large bowl.
7. Drizzle the dressing over the salad and toss to coat well.
8. Serve garnished with the dried basil.

Ingredient Tip: Add some fresh cheese like feta to add more taste.

Substitution Tip: You can use any bean of your choice.

Prep	Portion	Cook
10 m	4	0 m

Per Serving

Calories 141; Fat 8.6 g; Sodium 260 mg; Carb 16.1g; Fiber 4.4g; Sugar 8.9g; Protein 3g

TYRRHENIAN SEA STYLE SALAD

- 1 medium head of iceberg lettuce, washed, dried, and cut into pieces
- 4 medium tomatoes, sliced
- 1 medium carrot, shredded
- 1 small cucumber, sliced
- 1 small green bell pepper, seeded and thinly sliced
- 1 small onion, cut into rings
- ½ cup pitted olives (black or green)
- Lemon wedges, for serving
- Fresh parsley, chopped, for garnish

For the dressing:

- 2 tbsp. extra-virgin olive oil
- 2 tbsp. balsamic vinegar or red wine vinegar
- Kosher Salt and pepper, to taste

Directions:

1. Whisk dressing ingredients together in a small bowl and set aside.
2. Arrange the lettuce on a serving platter and add the tomatoes, carrot, cucumber, green bell pepper, onion, and olives.
3. Drizzle with the dressing.
4. Serve with lemon wedges and garnish with chopped parsley.

Ingredient Tip: Replace iceberg lettuce with crisp lettuce.

Prep	Portion	Cook
2h 10 m	4	0 m

Per Serving

Calories 141; Fat 8.6 g; Sodium 260 mg; Carb 16.1g; Fiber 4.4g; Sugar 8.9g; Protein 3g

BEAN SALAD

- 1 (15-ounce) can of fava beans, drained and rinsed
- 1 (15-ounce) can of chickpeas, drained and rinsed
- 1 (15½-ounce) can white beans, drained and rinsed
- ¼ cup flat-leaf parsley, chopped
- 3 tbsp. extra-virgin olive oil
- 2 cloves garlic, minced
- 1 lemon, squeezed
- Kosher salt and black pepper, to taste

Directions:

1. Carefully combine all ingredients in a bowl.
2. Refrigerate for 2 hours to marinate.
3. Top with fresh cilantro. Serve and enjoy!

Substitution Tip: Add chili flakes for a hint of heat.

Prep	Portion	Cook	Per Serving
10 m	4	7 m	Calories 303; Fat 18 g; Sat Fat: 7.4 g; Carb 16g; Protein: 20g

GREEK TZATZIKI SAUCE CHICKEN SALAD

- 3 tsp dried oregano
- 2 tbsp extra-virgin olive oil
- 1 tbsp red wine vinegar
- 4 ounces boneless chicken breasts
- 1 tsp ground black pepper
- 1 tbsp lemon juice
- 1 tsp kosher salt
- 1 cup English cucumbers, diced
- 6 cups lettuce
- 1 cup feta cheese, diced
- 1 cup tomatoes, diced
- ½ cup red onion, diced
- 1 cup pita chips, crushed
- Tzatziki sauce:
- 1 tbsp white wine vinegar
- ¾ tsp kosher salt
- 8 ounces Greek yogurt
- 1 clove of garlic, minced
- ⅔ cup English cucumber, grated
- 1 tbsp lemon juice
- ¾ tsp ground black pepper
- 2 tsp dried dill
- A pinch of sugar

Directions:

1. Heat the oil in a skillet over medium heat and add the chicken, salt, oregano, and black pepper.
2. Cook for five minutes.
3. Reduce the heat to low, add the lemon juice and vinegar and simmer for five minutes.
4. Continue cooking until the chicke is done. When the chicken is ready, remove the pan from the heat and set it aside.
5. Combine the tomatoes, pita chips chicken, lettuce, cucumber, and onions in a large bowl. Mix and set aside. The salad is ready.
6. Whisk yogurt, cucumber, garlic, lemon juice, vinegar, dill, salt, pepper, and sugar in another bowl. Mix well. Th sauce is ready.

Serving tip: Pour the dressing over the salad and serve with the cooked chicken.

Substitution tip: Marinate the chicken ahead of time for a tastier result.

Prep	Portion	Cook	Per Serving
10 m	2	35 m	Calories 353; Fat 13 g; Sat Fat: 1.4 g; Carb 55g; Protein: 6g

AUTUMN PUMPKIN RISOTTO

- 1 small pumpkin
- 1 tbsp extra virgin olive oil
- 1 cup of water
- 1/2 cup uncooked brown basmati rice
- 1/8 tsp ground cardamom
- 1/8 tsp ground cinnamon
- 1/4 tsp turmeric powder
- 1/4 tsp kosher salt
- 2 tbsp raisins
- 3 chopped dried apricots
- 1/4 cup lightly toasted pecans, chopped
- 1/8 tsp ground cumin

Directions:

1. Preheat the oven to 400°F, with the rack in the center. Peel and cut the squash before cutting it into 6 wedges. Discard the insides of the squash. Place the pumpkin wedges in a large bowl and toss to coat with the olive oil. Fan out the pumpkin wedges on a clean baking sheet and bake for 35 to 40 minutes, or until the wedges are fork-tender.
2. While the squash is cooking in the oven, bring the water and rice to a boil. Once the rice boils, lower the heat and cook covered for 20-25 minutes, or until the rice is well cooked. When the rice is well cooked, stir in the cardamom, cinnamon, turmeric, salt, raisins, apricots, and pecans.

Spread the rice on a serving plate and top with the roasted pumpkin segments. Sprinkle with cumin and serve hot.

Prep	Portion	Cook	Per Serving
10 m	8	0 m	Calories 313; Fat 29 g; Sat Fat: 6.4 g; Carb 10g; Protein: 5g

AVOCADO SALAD

- 2 English cucumbers, sliced
- ¼ pound tomatoes, cut into small pieces
- ¼ red onion, sliced
- ½ cup Kalamata olives, sliced
- ¼ cup fresh parsley, chopped
- 3 avocados, peeled, drained, and sliced
- 1 cup feta cheese, crumbled
- ½ cup extra virgin olive oil
- ½ cup red wine vinegar
- 2 cloves of garlic, minced
- 1 tbsp dried oregano
- 2 tsp sugar
- 1 tsp kosher salt
- 1 tsp ground black pepper

Directions:

1. Mix the tomatoes, parsley, onions, cucumbers, avocado, and olives in a large bowl. Set aside.
2. Whisk vinegar, sugar, olive oil, salt, oregano, garlic, and pepper in a jar.
3. Close the lid and shake to make an emulsified mixture.
4. You can add salt, black pepper, and sugar to adjust the taste according to your preference. The dressing is now ready!
5. Transfer the dressing to the salad bowl and mix well.
6. Serve.

Serving tip: Garnish with crumbled feta cheese.

Substitution tip: Avoid using mushy avocados.

Prep	Portion	Cook	Per Serving
20 m	4	0 m	Calories 361; Fat 21 g; Sat Fat: 4.6g; Carb 35g; Protein: 9g

CAULIFLOWER AND FARRO SALAD

For the salad

- ¾ cup of pearl farro
- Kosher salt, to taste
- 2 tbsp extra-virgin olive oil
- ½ medium red onion, thinly sliced
- ¼ cup fresh parsley, chopped
- 1 medium head of cauliflower, cut into bite-sized florets
- 2 ounces Parmesan cheese, shavings

For the dressing

- 2 tbsp fresh lemon juice
- 3 tbsp extra virgin olive oil
- 1 tbsp tahini paste
- ½ tsp kosher salt
- 1 small clove of minced garlic

Directions:

1. Heat a frying pan over medium heat. Toast the farro for about 5 minutes or until nutty and browned, shaking the pan occasionally.
2. Add water until the farro is covered about an inch, sprinkle with salt, and bring to a boil.
3. Cook for about 25 minutes until farro is tender but still chewy.
4. Drain the farro with a fine-mesh strainer.
5. Transfer farro to a large bowl and set aside to cool slightly.
6. Heat the olive oil in a skillet over medium-high heat and cook the cauliflower for about 6 minutes, stirring often.
7. Add the onion and sauté for about 3 minutes.
8. Remove from heat and set aside.
9. For the dressing: In a bowl, whisk all the dressing ingredients until well combined.
10. Add the farro, dressing, and cauliflower mixture to a large serving bowl and stir to coat everything well.
11. Serve with a garnish of parsley and Parmesan cheese.

Serving Tip: Accompany your favorite main dish.

Substitution tip: You can also add rosemary to this salad.

Prep	Portion	Cook	Per Serving
10 m	2	0 m	Calories: Calories 96; Fat 7g; Sat Fat: 0.9 g; Carb 8g; Protein: 2g

SUMMERTIME TOMATO SALAD

- 2 medium tomatoes, cut into wedges
- ½ of a small red onion, peeled and sliced
- ½ tsp. minced garlic
- ¼ cup chopped fresh parsley
- ¼ cup chopped dill, fresh
- ¼ tsp. salt
- ¼ tsp. ground black pepper
- ¼ tsp. ground sumac
- 1 tbsp. extra virgin olive oil
- 1 tsp. lemon juice
- ½ tsp. white wine vinegar

Directions

1. Take a large bowl, add the tomatoes, onion, parsley, dill, and garlic, and stir until mixed.
2. Then add the salt, black pepper, sumac, lemon juice, vinegar, and oil and toss until well combined.
3. Divide the salad between two bowls and serve.

Prep	Portion	Cook	Per Serving
10 m	6	0 m	Calories 413; Fat 28 g; Sat Fat: 4 g; Carb 16g; Protein: 29g

SALMON SALAD WITH PECANS

- 6 cups mixed greens (spinach, kale and chard)
- 2 large oranges, peeled and cut into pieces
- 2 red grapefruits, peeled and cut into pieces
- 1 avocado, peeled, pitted and cut into pieces
- 2 cans of boneless, skinless salmon, drained
- ½ cup pecans
- ½ cup pesto vinaigrette

Directions:

1. Arrange the vegetables on a large serving platter and top with the oranges, grapefruits, avocado, salmon, and pecans.
2. Drizzle the salad with the vinaigrette and serve.

Serving tip: Top with chopped cilantro.

Substitution tip: Replace pecans with sunflower or pumpkin seeds.

Prep
10 m

Portion
15

Cook
30-35m

Per Serving

Calories: 128; Total fat: 10.6g; Saturated fat: 1.8g; Carb: 1.2g; Protein: 4.1g; Fiber: 4.5g

THE ORIGINAL ITALIAN STYLE BAKED BREAD

- 1/4 cup ground chia seeds
- 1/4 cup psyllium powder
- 1/2 cup coconut flour
- 1/2 cup packed flax meal
- 1/2 tsp. baking soda
- 1/2 tsp. white pepper
- 1/2 tsp. Kosher salt
- 1/2 cup extra virgin olive oil
- 2 tbsp. crushed garlic
- 1 tbsp. chopped rosemary
- 1 tbsp. crushed oregano
- Whites of 8 large eggs
- 1 tbsp. white wine vinegar
- 1 cup lukewarm water

Directions:

1. Set oven to preheat to 285°F, with rack in the center of the oven—Line a large baking sheet with foil.
2. In a large bowl, whisk together the chia seeds, psyllium powder, coconut flour, flax meal, baking soda, white pepper, and salt. Set aside.
3. Whisk the olive oil, garlic, rosemary, and oregano in a small glass bowl. Set aside.
4. In a third clean bowl, beat the egg whites until soft peaks form, pouring in the vinegar gradually as you beat to help keep the peaks in place.
5. Using a mixer, add the warm water to the flour and process while gradually pouring half of the oil mixture into the bowl. As soon as the oil is incorporated, slowly add half of the beaten egg whites. Add the remaining egg whites while the mixer runs until all ingredients form a dough.
6. Transfer the dough to the prepared pan and use your hands to press the dough onto the pan. Gently press the dough with your fingers, creating small pockets. Take the remaining olive oil mixture and use a basting brush to coat the top of the dough. Bake for 30-35 minutes, or until the bread is crisp and golden brown.
7. Transfer the baked bread to a wire rack and let it rest for 5 minutes before cutting it into 15 pieces and serving.

Ingredient Tip: Add some green olives sliced to add more flavor to your bread.

Suggestion Tip: Baked bread can be stored on the counter for up to 3 days or frozen in an airtight container for no more than 3 months.

Prep
5 m

Portion
4

Cook
20 m

Per Serving

Calories: 224; Total fat: 5g; Saturated fat: 2g; Carb: 40g; Protein: 6g; Sodium: 922mg; Fiber: 6g

GREEK-STYLE MASHED POTATOES

- 2 lbs. russet potatoes, peeled and diced (1-inch cubes)
- 1 1/2 tsp. Kosher salt (divided)
- 2 spring onions, thinly sliced
- 2 tbsp. extra virgin olive oil
- 1/2 cup whole milk (more if needed)
- 1/2 cup plain Greek yogurt
- 1 tbsp. fresh dill, chopped

Directions:

1. Fill a large pot with water to cover the potatoes, and bring to a boil, along with 1 tsp. salt. Boil the potatoes for about 15-20 minutes, or until all the potatoes are softened. Strain the potatoes through a strainer placed over the sink.
2. Transfer the cooked potatoes to a large bowl and mash them with spring onions, olive oil, milk, yogurt, and 1/2 tsp. salt. Add more milk if necessary to reach desired consistency.
3. Spoon into a serving dish and garnish with the dill before serving

Ingredient tip: You can add some sliced onion and put the salad in the fridge for 30 minutes before serving.

Prep	Portion	Cook	Per Serving
10 m	2	0 m	Calories 139; Fat 5 g; Sat Fat: 0.7 g; Carb 26g; Protein: 5g

GREEK-STYLE CUCUMBER SALAD

- 1 cup diced tomatoes
- 4 tbsp. diced cucumber
- ¼ cup chopped parsley, fresh
- ¼ tsp. salt
- ¼ tsp. ground black pepper
- ¼ tsp. ground sumac
- 1 ½ tsp. extra virgin olive oil
- 1 tsp. lemon juice

Directions

1. Take a medium bowl, add tomato, cucumber, salt, and parsley, toss until well mixed, and then set aside for 5 minutes.
2. Then add sumac and oil, and then toss until combined.
3. Divide the salad between two bowls and then serve.

Prep	Portion	Cook	Per Serving
5 m	6	0 m	Calories 287; Fat 26 g; Sat Fat: 7.6 g; Carb 8g; Protein: 6g

CHORIATIKI SALAD

- 1/4 cup capers
- 16 pitted black olives
- 1 small red onion, sliced
- 1 medium green bell pepper, sliced
- 1 large English cucumber, diced
- 4-5 heirloom tomatoes, chopped
- 7 oz. whole feta cheese (2 wheels)
- 1 tsp dried oregano
- 1/2 cup extra-virgin olive oil
- Freshly ground black pepper
- ¼ tsp. Sea salt

Directions:

1. In a large serving bowl, bring together capers, olives, onions, peppers, cucumbers, and tomatoes. Crumble one wheel feta into the bowl and toss together with half of the oregano and half of the olive oil.
2. Place the remaining whole feta round on top of the salad and sprinkle with the remaining oregano and olive oil. Before serving, season the salad with pepper and salt. The salad can be stored for up to one day, but it is best served fresh.

Substitution tip: replace feta with goat cheese.

Prep	Portion	Cook	Per Serving
10 m	6	0 m	Calories 91; Fat 4.3g; Sodium 130mg; Carb 11.4g; Fiber 0.5g; Sugar 5.4g; Protein 3.5g

SUMMERTIME WATERMELON SALAD

- 6 cups mixed salad, torn up
- 3 cups watermelon, seeded and cubed
- ½ cup onion, sliced
- 1 tbsp. extra-virgin olive oil
- ⅓ cup feta cheese, crumbled
- Ground black pepper, to taste

Directions:

1. In a large bowl, mix all ingredients.
2. Toss to combine everything well.
3. Allow cooling before serving.

Ingredient Tip: Serve with your favorite barbequed meat.
Substitution Tip: For a creamier result, add avocado slices.

Prep
5 m

Portion
4

Cook
0 m

Per Serving

Calories: 343; Total fat: 28g; Saturated fat: 4g; Carb: 6g; Protein: 21g; Sodium: 1,217mg; Fiber: 2g

BLUE ZONE TUNA SALAD

- 1 tbsp. Sea salt
- 3 tbsp. white wine vinegar
- 1/4 cup extra-virgin olive oil
- 1 tsp. crushed garlic
- 1 medium red bell pepper, seeded and diced
- 1 cup pitted green olives
- 6 ounces canned tuna in olive oil, well-drained
- 1 bag of mixed salad

Directions:

1. Place the salt, vinegar, and oil in a large bowl. Whisk until well combined.
2. Gently stir in the garlic, peppers, and olives. Add the drained tuna and mix until all ingredients are well combined.
3. Serve the cooled tuna mixture on a bed of mixed salad.

Prep
10 m

Portion
2 Servings

Cook
0 m

Per Serving

Calories: 62.5; Fat: 4.9 g; Sat. Fat: 0.7 g; Carb: 4.8 g; Protein: 1 g; Fiber: 1.2 g

FRESH CUCUMBER MEDITERRANEAN SALAD

- 1 cup diced tomatoes
- 4 tbsp. diced cucumber
- ¼ cup chopped parsley, fresh
- ¼ tsp. salt
- ¼ tsp. ground black pepper
- ¼ tsp. ground sumac
- 1 ½ tsp. extra-virgin olive oil
- 1 tsp. lemon juice

Directions

1. Take a medium bowl, add tomato, cucumber, salt, and parsley, toss until well mixed, and then set aside for 5 minutes.
2. Then add sumac and oil, and then toss until combined.
3. Divide the salad between two bowls and then serve.

Prep
20 m

Portion
8

Cook
10 m

Per Serving

Calories: 299; Fat: 10.3g; Sat fat: 4g; Carb: 42.1g; Fiber: 5.5g; Sugar: 6.7g; Protein: 11.7g

PASTA SALAD WITH ARUGULA AND ASPARAGUS

- 1 pound fresh asparagus, cut into small pieces
- 1 pound whole-wheat pasta
- 1 tbsp. red wine vinegar
- 2 tbsp. lemon zest, grated
- 2 large handfuls of fresh arugula
- ⅔ cup feta cheese, crumbled
- Black pepper, to taste
- 3 tbsp. fresh lemon juice
- 1 tbsp. extra-virgin olive oil
- ¼ cup fresh basil, julienned
- ¼ cup pine nuts, toasted

Directions:

1. In a large pot of salted water, cook whole wheat pasta for about 10 minutes or al dente.
2. Add the asparagus and mix well.
3. Remove the pot from the heat and transfer the pasta and asparagus to a colander.
4. Run cold water over the pasta and asparagus and drain well.
5. Stir in the pasta, vinegar, asparagus, olive oil, lemon zest, and lemon juice, and mix well.
6. Move the pasta mixture to a large serving bowl.
7. Stir in the arugula, feta cheese, basil, pine nuts, and black pepper.
8. Gently stir to coat well and serve immediately.

Tip: Top with a few nuts before serving, if you like.

Substitution Tip: You can use fresh parsley instead of basil.

Poultry

TURKEY MEATBALLS WITH FETA CHEESE

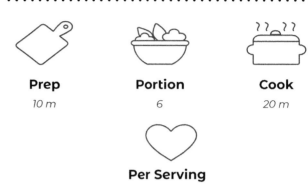

Prep
10 m

Portion
6

Cook
20 m

Per Serving

Calories 290; Fat 16g; Sat Fat: 6.1g; Carb 2g; Protein: 34g

Ingredients:

- *1 egg, lightly beaten*
- *2 pounds of ground turkey*
- *4 ounces feta cheese, crumbled*
- *1 tbsp chopped fresh mint*
- *¼ tsp cumin*
- *½ tsp onion powder*
- *½ cup almond meal*
- *¼ cup chopped fresh parsley*
- *1 cup chopped spinach*
- *½ tsp oregano*
- *½ tsp pepper*
- *½ tsp Sea salt*

Directions:

1. *Preheat the oven to 450° F.*
2. *Add ground turkey and remaining ingredients to a large bowl and mix until well combined.*
3. *Form balls with the meat mixture and arrange them on the baking sheet.*
4. *Bake for 20 minutes.*

Serving Tip: Allow to cool completely and serve.
Substitution Tip: crumbled goat cheese can be used instead of feta cheese.

	Prep 10 m	**Portion** 4	**Cook** 15 m	**Per Serving** *Calories 607; Fat 14g; Sat Fat: 2g; Carb 3g; Protein: 51g*

MEDITERRANEAN MARINATED GRILLED CHICKEN

- 2 lb. chicken breasts, skinless and boneless
- ½ tsp red pepper flakes
- 1 tsp dried oregano
- 2 tbsp of fresh lemon juice
- 1 tbsp minced garlic
- 3 tbsp extra virgin olive oil
- 1 tbsp balsamic vinegar
- ½ tsp onion powder
- ½ tsp of pepper
- ½ tsp Kosher salt

Directions:

1. Add chicken and other ingredients to a zip-lock bag. Close the bag and place it in the refrigerator overnight.
2. Preheat the grill.
3. Place marinated chicken on the grill and cook for 5-7 minutes on each side.

Serving tip: Allow to cool completely and serve.

Substitution tip: Add seasonings of your choice.

Prep 5 m	**Portion** 4	**Cook** 30 m	**Per Serving** *Calories 311; Fat 10g; Sat Fat: 2.7g; Carb 39g; Protein: 16g*

CHICKEN GYROS WRAPPED IN LETTUCE

- 1 1/2 lbs. boneless, skinned chicken breasts
- 1/2 tsp white pepper
- 1/2 tsp kosher salt
- 1/2 tsp dried thyme
- 1/2 tsp dried oregano
- 1/2 tsp ground cumin
- 1 tbsp crushed garlic
- 2 tbsp freshly squeezed lemon juice
- 1 lemon, cut into zest
- 8 outer leaves of romaine lettuce
- Tahini sauce

- 4 thin spears of dill pickles
- Very thinly sliced red onion
- 1 heirloom tomato, sliced

Directions:

1. Place the chicken breasts on a wooden cutting board and cover them with wax paper. Pound the breasts with a wooden mallet until they are about 1.5 cm thick before cutting them into 6 strips.
2. Whisk together the pepper, salt, thyme, oregano, cumin, garlic, lemon juice, and lemon zest in a large bowl. Add the chicken strips and toss to coat.

Cover the bowl with plastic wrap and chill overnight or for at least 30 minutes.

3. When the chicken is well chilled, preheat the oven to low, with the rack about 6 inches away from the grill. Place the chicken strips on a foil-covered baking sheet and bake them in the oven for 7 minutes or until the chicken is well done.
4. Arrange the lettuce leaves on a plate and top each leaf with a generous amount of tahini sauce, followed by the dill leaves, red onions, and tomato slices. Divide the cooked chicken among the leaves, fold and serve.

Prep 10 m	**Portion** 4	**Cook** 20 m	**Per Serving** *Calories 517; Fat 24g; Sat Fat: 5.2g; Carb 52g; Protein: 21g*

GRILLED CHICKEN WITH OREGANO

- ½ cup lemon juice
- ½ cup of extra virgin olive oil
- 3 tbsp minced garlic
- 2 tsp dried oregano
- 1 tsp red pepper flakes
- 1 tsp of salt
- 2 pounds of boneless, skinless chicken breasts

Directions:

1. Combine the garlic, lemon juice, olive oil, oregano, red pepper flakes, and salt in a medium bowl.
2. Split one chicken breast horizontally to make two thin pieces. Repeat with the rest of the chicken breasts.
3. Place the chicken in the bowl with the marinade and let it rest for at least 10 minutes before cooking.
4. Place a skillet over high heat and add a little oil.
5. Cook each side of the breasts for 10 minutes, turning regularly.
6. Serve hot.

Serving tip: Serve with lemon wedges.

Substitution tip: Omit the red pepper flakes for a milder taste.

Prep	Portion	Cook	Per Serving
10 m	4	15 m	Calories: 280; Total fat: 17g; Carb: 10g; Protein: 23g; Sodium: 251mg; Fiber: 2g

GROUND TURKEY

- 2 tbsp. avocado oil
- 1 pound lean ground turkey
- 2 tbsp. crushed garlic
- 1 medium red bell pepper, seeded and diced
- 1 small shallot, chopped
- 1/2 tsp. ground cumin
- 1/2 tsp. ground cinnamon
- Freshly ground black pepper
- 1/4 tsp. kosher salt
- 2 tbsp. hummus
- 1/4 cup chicken broth
- 1 lemon, finely peeled
- 1 tbsp. lemon juice
- Fresh parsley, chopped, for garnish

Directions:

1. Heat 1 tbsp. oil in a large skillet over medium-high heat. When the oil is nice and hot, add the ground turkey, and fry for about 5 minutes in a single layer, without stirring. After 5 minutes, turn the meat over with a spatula and stir to separate all the pieces. Scrape into a bowl and set aside.

2. Return the skillet to medium-low heat and add the remaining oil. When the oil is nice and hot, sauté the garlic, peppers, and scallions for about 5 minutes, or until the vegetables are tender. Stir in the cumin and cinnamon for about 30 seconds before adding the ground turkey to the skillet, along with a large pinch of pepper, salt, hummus, chicken broth, lemon zest, and lemon juice. Stir for 5 minutes.

3. Serve the ground turkey on wraps of your choice, garnished with fresh parsley.

Ingredient tip: You can add some mushrooms for more flavor.

Prep	Portion	Cook	Per Serving
5 m	2	15 m	Calories: 245.2 calories; Fat: 9.5 g; Sat. Fat: 4.1 g; Carb: 8.5 g; Protein: 31 g; Fiber: 1.5 g

MEDITERRANEAN CHICKEN SKILLET WITH MUSHROOMS

- 5-ounce portobello mushrooms, sliced
- 1/2 of a large white onion, peeled, cut into round slices
- 1 pound chicken breast, cut into strips
- 1/4 tsp. sea salt, divided
- 1/4 tsp. ground black pepper, divided
- 1/2 tsp. dried thyme
- 1 1/2 tbsp. extra-virgin olive oil, divided
- 1/2 tbsp. balsamic vinegar
- 3 tbsp. white wine
- 1/4 cup vegetable broth
- 1-ounce Parmesan cheese, sliced

Directions

1. Take a large bowl, place chicken strips in it, add salt, black pepper, and thyme, pour in oil, vinegar, and white wine, toss until well coated, and set aside until required.

2. Take a medium skillet pan, place it over medium heat, add oil, and when hot, add onion and cook for 1 minute until begin to tender.

3. Add mushroom, salt, and black pepper, pour into the vegetable broth, cook for 5 minutes until softened, and when done, transfer the mushroom mixture into a bowl.

4. Then add marinated chicken into the pan, cook for 5 minutes, return the mushroom mixture into the pan, and cook for 3 minutes until thoroughly hot.

5. When done, place the cooked mushroom chicken into a serving plate, place parmesan slices on the side, and serve.

Prep	Portion	Cook	Per Serving
15 m	4	40 m	Calories: 355; Fat: 14g; Sat fat: 3.7g; Carb: 4.7g; Fiber: 1.4g; Sugar: 3g; Protein: 50.3g

CHICKEN BREAST TOMATO BRUSCHETTA

- 4 (6-ounce) chicken breasts
- Olive oil cooking spray
- Salt and black pepper, to taste
- 1/4 cup fresh basil leaves, chopped
- 1 tsp. balsamic vinegar
- 5 small tomatoes, chopped
- 1 clove of garlic, minced
- 1 tsp. extra-virgin olive oil

Directions:

1. Preheat the oven to 375degreesF and grease a baking sheet with olive oil cooking spray.

2. Season the chicken breasts with salt and black pepper.

3. Arrange the chicken breasts in a single layer in the baking dish.

4. Cover the baking dish and bake for about 40 minutes.

5. Meanwhile, add the tomatoes, garlic, basil, vinegar, oil, and salt to a bowl.

6. Mix well and refrigerate until ready to use.

7. Remove chicken breasts from the oven and transfer to serving plates.

8. Serve topped with the tomato mixture.

Substitution Tip: You can use any variety of tomatoes you like. You can replace chicken breast with turkey breast.

Prep	Portion	Cook	Per Serving
5 m	4	30 m	Calories 607; Fat 38g; Sat Fat: 7g; Carb 10g; Protein: 55g

AUTUMN CHICKEN WITH CABBAGE

- Zest of 1/2 small lemon
- 2 tbsp extra virgin olive oil
- ¼ tsp Kosher salt
- Freshly ground black pepper
- 2 large chicken thighs, diced
- 4 tbsp avocado oil (divided)
- 1 tsp crushed garlic
- 1/2 small shallot, diced
- 1 cup champignon mushrooms, sliced
- 1 cup reduced-sodium chicken broth
- 1/2 cup whole cream
- 2 tbsp fresh tarragon, chopped
- 1 tbsp freshly squeezed lemon juice
- 3/4 to 1 cup water (divided)
- 3 oz. slices of bacon, cut into strips
- 1 small head of savoy cabbage, seeded and sliced

Directions:

1. Whisk together the lemon zest, olive oil, and a pinch of salt and pepper in a large bowl. Add the chicken cubes and toss to coat. Cover the bowl and chill for at least two hours or overnight.

2. In a large skillet over medium heat, heat 2 tbsp avocado oil before adding the garlic and scallions and sautéing for 3 to 5 minutes, or until the scallions become translucent. Pour the bowl of chicken cubes and the sauce into the skillet and cook for 8 minutes, stirring at regular intervals to prevent burning.

3. Add the mushrooms and cook for 4-5 minutes before adding the chicken stock and bringing the pan to a boil. Simmer for 5 minutes, stirring. Add the cream and cook for another 5 minutes. Add the tarragon and lemon juice to the skillet and stir before seasoning to taste with salt and pepper. Transfer the skillet to a wooden cutting board and keep warm.

4. Add 1/2 cup water to a clean skillet and the bacon strips. Bring the bacon to a boil over medium-high heat and simmer for 5 to 8 minutes, or until the water has reduced and the bacon has become crispy. Using a slotted spoon, transfer the crispy bacon to a plate and cover it with aluminum foil.

5. Wipe out the skillet and add the remaining avocado oil. Heat the oil over medium-high heat; when the oil is hot, add the cabbage and sauté for about 30 seconds. Pour in the remaining water and season with salt and pepper. Put a lid on the pan and simmer the cabbage for 8 to 12 minutes, or until well cooked but still crisp.

6. Transfer the skillet to a wooden cutting board and stir in the crispy bacon. Serve the cooked chicken on a bed of crispy bacon and cabbage noodles.

Prep	Portion	Cook	Per Serving (1 Meatball)
10 m	20 Makes	30 m	Calories 71; Fat 5g; Sat Fat: 1.3g; Carb 1g; Protein: 5g

CHICKEN DRUMSTICKS

- ½ tsp. fresh thyme
- ¼ tsp. sweet paprika
- 1 red onion, thinly sliced
- 3 tomatoes, chopped
- Kosher salt and black pepper, to taste
- ½ cup fresh parsley, chopped
- 1 tsp. dried oregano
- 1 pound ground chicken
- ½ tsp. minced garlic cloves
- 1 raw egg
- ¼ cup Parmesan cheese, grated
- 2 tbsp. extra virgin olive oil.

Directions:

1. Preheat the oven to 375degrees F.

2. Coat a pan with a bit of extra virgin olive oil and set it aside.

3. Mix tomatoes with kosher salt and onions in a large bowl.

4. Add half of your fresh thyme and drizzle a little extra virgin olive oil again.

5. Transfer this mixture to your skillet and use a spoon to distribute it evenly.

6. Add the ground chicken to a bowl and add the egg, Parmesan cheese, a little extra virgin olive oil, oregano, paprika, garlic, the remaining thyme, chopped parsley, and black pepper.

7. Mix the mixture well and form chicken patties about 1 1/2 inches in size.

8. Arrange the patties in the prepared pan.

9. Bake in the preheated oven for about 30 minutes.

10. Your meatballs should turn golden brown when ready.

11. Serve and enjoy.

Tip: Serve with tomato sauce.

Ingredient tip: Add a pinch of chili for spice. You can replace the tomato sauce with tzatziki sauce.

Prep
10 m

Portion
4

Cook
20-25m

Per Serving
Calories 438; Fat 33g; Sat Fat: 6.7g; Carb 9g; Protein: 26g

ITALIAN-STYLE TURKEY PATTIES IN GREEN SAUCE

- 3/4 cup extra virgin olive oil
- 2 tbsp freshly squeezed lemon juice
- 3 tbsp balsamic vinegar
- 2 tbsp crushed garlic
- 4 pieces of canned anchovies, drained
- 2 tbsp capers
- 1/4 cup fresh mint leaves, chopped
- 2 cups fresh parsley leaves, packed
- 1 cup fresh basil leaves, packed
- ½ tsp Kosher salt
- Freshly ground black pepper
- 1 tbsp extra virgin avocado oil (if needed)
- 1 tsp fresh thyme leaves
- 1 small shallot, chopped
- 3 tbsp coconut flour
- 1 lemon, cut into zest
- 1 large free-range egg
- 1 lb. lean ground turkey

Directions:

1.	In a food processor, grind the olive oil, lemon juice, vinegar, garlic, anchovies, capers, mint leaves, parsley, and basil at high speed until a lump-free paste is obtained. Season with salt and pepper before pouring half the mixture into a bowl and covering it to cool while you prepare the rest of the dish. The rest of the sauce can be stored in the refrigerator in an airtight container for no more than 2 weeks.

2.	In a small skillet over medium heat, heat the avocado oil before sautéing the thyme leaves and scallions for about 3 minutes, or until the scallions begin to soften. Remove the pan from the heat and scrape the scallions and thyme into a large serving bowl. Allow cooling slightly.

3.	When the scallions have cooled slightly, add the coconut flour, zest, egg, and turkey, plus 1/2 tsp each salt and pepper, to the bowl. Use clean hands to properly combine all ingredients. Form the meat into 16 patties and fry them in groups of four or more (using the same pan used to fry the scallions), about 8 minutes per side. Transfer the cooked patties to a serving plate and keep warm. Repeat with the remaining patties, adding a little avocado oil to the pan if necessary.

4.	Serve the cooked patties with a side of cooled "salsa verde" (green sauce) for dipping.

Prep
10 m

Portion
6

Cook
1h 10 m

Per Serving
736; Fat 19g; Sat Fat: 3.6g; Carb 9g; Protein: 62g

CACCIATORE ITALIAN-STYLE CHICKEN

- 1 cup boiling water
- 1/2 oz. dried porcini mushrooms
- 2 tbsp. avocado oil
- 12 boneless chicken thighs, skinned and fat removed
- 1 large fennel bulb, cored, cut in half and thinly sliced
- 1 large shallot, split in half and sliced thinly
- 1 large green bell pepper, stripped of seeds and cut into rings
- 1 tsp fresh thyme leaves, chopped
- 2 tbsp finely grated orange zest
- 1 tbsp fresh rosemary, chopped
- 3 tbsp crushed garlic
- 3 tbsp balsamic vinegar
- 1/2 tbsp kosher salt
- 2 tbsp tomato paste
- 3/4 cup dry white wine

Directions:

1.	Preheat the oven to 350°F, with the rack in the center.

2.	Place the boiling water and mushrooms in a large bowl and let them soak on the counter for 20 minutes.

3.	Meanwhile, heat the olive oil in a large skillet over medium-high heat before adding the chicken thighs and browning them on all sides. If necessary, cook the chicken in several rounds to avoid overcrowding the pan. Transfer the cooked thighs to a large casserole dish.

4.	Lower the heat and add the fennel, scallions, and peppers to the same skillet, sautéing for about 5 minutes, or until the vegetables are fork tender. Add the thyme, zest, rosemary, and garlic. Sauté for 30 seconds before adding the vinegar and sautéing for another minute.

5.	Finely chop the soaked mushrooms before adding them to the pan, along with the soaking water, salt, tomato paste, and wine.

6.	When the sauce begins to boil, carefully pour the contents of the pan over the thighs in the casserole dish. Cover the dish with aluminum foil and bake for 45 minutes.

7.	Allow the cooked thighs to rest on the counter for 5-10 minutes before serving hot.

Ingredient Tip: Serve on a bed of rice or mashed potatoes for a complete dish. You can add black olives to add more taste.

Prep
10 m

Portion
4

Cook
50 m

Per Serving
Calories 364; Fat 14g; Sat Fat: 2.4g; Carb 3g; Protein: 54g

CHICKEN AND RADISH SALAD

- 4 boneless, skinless chicken breasts
- ½ tsp Kosher salt
- Freshly ground black pepper
- 2/3 cup Moroccan chermoula
- 1 cup fresh parsley leaves, chopped
- 1/4 cup red onion, thinly sliced
- 1 English cucumber, thinly sliced
- 12 small radishes, thinly sliced
- 2 tbsp extra virgin olive oil
- 1 tbsp freshly squeezed lemon juice
- 1 tbsp lightly toasted sesame seeds

Directions:

1. Place the chicken breasts on a wooden cutting board and, with a sharp knife, make a few small slits. Rub the breasts with a generous pinch of salt and pepper before placing them in a bowl. Coat the breasts with chermoula and chill covered for at least an hour or overnight.

2. Preheat the oven to 400°F, with the rack in the center.

3. Place the marinated chicken and the marinade in an ovenproof dish and bake for 45 to 50 minutes, or until the chicken is cooked through. Allow the chicken to rest on the work surface while you prepare the salad.

4. In a large bowl, gently mix the parsley, onion, cucumber, and radishes. Add the olive oil, lemon juice, and 1/4 tsp of each salt and pepper to the bowl, stirring until all ingredients are evenly coated.

Serve the chicken on a bed of the radish salad and garnish with the sesame seeds before serving.

Prep
5 m

Portion
4

Cook
15 m

Per Serving
Calories 498; Fat 18g; Sat Fat: 3.3g; Carb 68g; Protein: 17g

GREEK-STYLE CHICKEN AND BARLEY

- 2 cups water
- 1 cup of raw, quick-cooking barley
- 3 tbsp avocado oil
- 1 lb. boneless, skinless chicken breasts, diced
- 1 medium shallot, chopped
- 1/3 tsp cayenne pepper
- 1/4 tsp white pepper
- 1/4 tsp Sea salt
- 1/2 tsp dried basil, chopped
- 1 tsp dried oregano, chopped
- 2 tbsp crushed garlic
- 2 medium zucchini, chopped
- 1 tbsp fresh flat-leaf parsley, chopped
- 1/4 cup Kalamata olives, pitted and cut in half
- 2 heirloom tomatoes, chopped

Directions:

1. Bring 2 cups of water to a boil over medium heat. When the water boils, turn the heat to medium-low and stir in the raw barley. Put a lid on the pot and simmer for 10 to 12 minutes until the barley is cooked, stirring occasionally. Remove the pot from the heat and let it cool for about 5 minutes.

2. Heat 2 tsp of oil in a large skillet over medium heat and fry the chicken cubes until well cooked. Transfer them to a bowl and cover with aluminum foil to keep warm.

3. Add 1 tsp of oil to the same pan and heat it. When the oil is hot, sauté the shallots for about 3 minutes, or until just softened. Stir in cayenne pepper, white pepper, salt, basil, oregano, garlic, and zucchini for a few minutes, until zucchini is softened.

4. Stir in the parsley, olives, tomatoes, and chicken. Serve on a bed of cooked barley.

Prep
10 m

Portion
2

Cook
25 m

Per Serving
Calories: 355 calories; Fat: 18.9 g; Sat. Fat: 5.9 g Carb: 10 g
Protein: 37.6 g; Fiber: 4.2 g

CHICKEN CAPRESE HASSELBACK

½ of a medium tomato, sliced
4 cups broccoli florets
8 ounces chicken breast, boneless
¼ tsp. salt, divided
¼ tsp. ground black pepper, divided
4 tbsp. pesto sauce
1 tbsp. extra-virgin olive oil
1 1/2 ounces mozzarella cheese, low-fat, sliced

Directions

1. Turn on the oven, set the temperature to 190 degrees C or 375 degrees F, and let it preheat.

2. Meanwhile, take a large baking sheet, grease it with oil, and set it aside until needed.

3. Place the chicken breast on a cutting board, make ½ inch deep cuts across the top, but do not cut through.

4. Season the chicken with salt and black pepper until well coated, and then stuff the cuts with tomato slices and mozzarella cheese.

5. Brush the pesto sauce over the chicken and transfer the chicken to the prepared baking sheet.

6. Take a large bowl, put in the broccoli florets, add the salt and black pepper, drizzle with the oil, and toss until well coated.

7. Add the prepared broccoli florets to the side of the chicken in the baking dish and then bake for 25 minutes, or until the chicken is fully cooked and the top turns golden brown.

8. When done, transfer the chicken breast to a cutting board and cut in half, divide the chicken pieces between two plates, add the roasted broccoli florets to the side and serve.

Prep
20 m + one night
for marinating

Portion
4

Cook
50 m

Per Serving
Calories: 634; Fat: 26.1g; Sat fat: 4.9g; Carb: 44.6g; Fiber:
6.2g; Sugar: 27.3g; Protein: 49.2g

CHICKEN AND DRIED FRUIT CASSEROLE

- 6 ounces dried plums, quartered
- 6 ounces of dried apricots, quartered
- 4 ounces of pitted black olives
- 2 cloves garlic, crushed
- Salt and black pepper, to taste
- ⅔ cup red wine vinegar
- 4 chicken thighs (6 ounces)
- ¾ cup white wine
- 2 ounces capers
- 2 tbsp. fresh oregano, chopped
- 1 bay leaf
- ¼ cup extra-virgin olive oil
- 3 tbsp. brown sugar

Directions:

1. For the marinade: In a large baking dish, add the apricots, olives, plums, capers, oregano, garlic, salt, black pepper, vinegar, bay leaf, and oil and mix well.

2. Add the chicken breasts and coat them generously with the marinade.

3. Cover the pan and refrigerate overnight.

4. Remove from refrigerator 1 hour before cooking and keep at room temperature.

5. Heat oven to 325degreesF.

6. Arrange chicken breasts on a baking sheet in a single layer.

7. Spread marinade evenly over chicken breasts and sprinkle with brown sugar.

8. Pour the white wine around the chicken breasts.

9. Bake for about 50 minutes and serve hot.

Ingredient tip: Serve with roasted asparagus.

Substitution tip: You can use honey instead of brown sugar.

Prep

10 m

Makes

20

Cook

30 m

Per Serving

Calories 79; Fat 4.6g; Sodium 74.7mg; Carb 4.1g; Fiber 0.4g;

Sugar 1.4g; Protein 7.8g

ITALIAN STYLE CHICKEN MEATBALLS

- 3 tomatoes, chopped
- Kosher salt and black pepper, to taste
- ½ cup fresh parsley, chopped
- 1 tsp. dried oregano
- ½ tsp. fresh thyme
- ¼ tsp. sweet paprika
- 1 red onion, thinly sliced
- 1 pound ground chicken
- ½ tsp. minced garlic cloves
- 1 raw egg
- ¼ cup Parmesan cheese, grated
- 2 tbsp. extra virgin olive oil.

Directions:

1. Preheat the oven to 375 degrees F.
2. Coat a pan with a bit of extra virgin olive oil and set it aside.
3. Mix tomatoes with kosher salt and onions in a large bowl.
4. Add half of your fresh thyme and drizzle a little extra virgin olive oil again.
5. Transfer this mixture to your skillet and use a spoon to distribute it evenly.
6. Add the ground chicken to a bowl and add the egg, Parmesan cheese, a little extra virgin olive oil, oregano, paprika, garlic, the remaining thyme, chopped parsley, and black pepper.
7. Mix the mixture well and form chicken patties about 1 1/2 inches in size.
8. Arrange the patties in the prepared pan.
9. Bake in the preheated oven for about 30 minutes.
10. Your meatballs should turn golden brown when ready.
11. Serve and enjoy.

Tip: Serve with tomato sauce.

Ingredient tip: Add a pinch of chili for spice.

Prep

10 m

Portion

8

Cook

40 m

Per Serving

Calories 281; Fat 8g; Sodium 413mg; Carb 14g; Fiber 3.3g;

Sugar 9.6g; Protein 39g

CACCIATORA-TUSCAN CHICKEN

- 2 tbsp. extra virgin olive oil
- 1 medium onion, chopped
- 3 tbsp. minced garlic
- 1 whole chicken, cut into 8 pieces
- 1 medium carrot, diced
- 1 medium potato, diced
- 1 medium red bell pepper, thinly sliced
- 2 cups stewed tomatoes
- 1 cup tomato sauce
- ½ cup green peas
- 1 tsp. dried thyme
- Salt and black pepper, if needed

Directions:

1. Place a large saucepan over medium-high heat.
2. Add the oil and allow it to heat.
3. Add the garlic and onion and cook for 2 minutes.
4. Add the chicken and cook for 7 minutes, stirring.
5. Add the carrots, red bell pepper, potato, stewed tomatoes, tomato sauce, green peas, and thyme and mix well.
6. Reduce the heat to low and simmer for 30 minutes. Season with salt and pepper.
7. Transfer to a serving dish and enjoy!

Ingredient Tip: Add chili for a spicier dish. Serve on a bed of rice or mashed potatoes for a complete dish. You can add black olives to add more taste.

Prep

10 m

Portion

6

Cook

8 h

Per Serving

Calories 373; Fat 21g; Sat Fat: 3.6g; Carb 8g; Protein: 27g

CHICKEN WITH ARTICHOKES

- *6 chicken thighs, skinless and boneless*
- *1 tsp dried basil*
- *1 tsp dried oregano*
- *14 pitted olives*
- *10 ounces frozen artichoke hearts*
- *14 ounces canned tomatoes, diced*
- *½ tsp garlic powder*
- *3 tbsp fresh lemon juice*
- *Pepper*
- *¼ tsp sea salt*

Directions:

1.   Season the chicken with pepper and salt and place it in the slow cooker.

2.   Pour the remaining ingredients over the chicken.

3.   Cover and simmer for 8 hours.

Serving tip: Allow to cool completely and serve.

Substitution tip: Add 1 small sliced onion.

Prep

25 m

Portion

4

Cook

25 m

Per Serving

Calories 179; Fat 6g; Sat Fat: 2g; Carb 13g; Protein: 19g

GREEK YOGURT CHICKEN WITH MINT

- *1 cup low-fat Greek yogurt*
- *1 onion, finely chopped*
- *1 tbsp fresh mint, chopped*
- *1 tsp chopped fresh dill*
- *1 tsp minced garlic*
- *1 tsp ground cumin*
- *A pinch of red pepper flakes*
- *4 boneless, skinless chicken breasts (3 ounces)*

Directions:

1.   In a medium-sized bowl, whisk together the yogurt, onion, mint, dill, garlic, cumin, and red pepper flakes until blended.

2.   Transfer ½ cup yogurt to a small bowl. Set aside, covered, in the refrigerator.

3.   Add chicken to the remaining yogurt mixture, turning to coat.

4.   Cover and place chicken in the refrigerator to marinate for 3 hours.

5.   preheat oven to 400°F.

6.   Transfer chicken breasts to a baking sheet and roast until chicken is cooked, 25 minutes.

7.   Serve with reserved yogurt and mint sauce.

Serving tip: Garnish with sprigs of rosemary.

Substitution tip: Substitute chicken breast for turkey breast.

Prep

10 m

Portion

6

Cook

18 m

Per Serving

Calories 342; Fat 24g; Sat Fat: 9.2g; Carb 2g; Protein: 26g

BAKED CHICKEN BREAST

- *2 pounds boneless chicken breast*
- *Salt and pepper, to taste*
- *1 tsp thyme*
- *1 sliced red onion*
- *1 tsp dried oregano*
- *1 tsp sweet paprika*
- *1 tbsp extra virgin olive oil*
- *2 cloves of garlic, minced*
- *1 tbsp lemon juice*
- *½ tsp sea salt*
- *Campari tomatoes, to taste*
- *A handful of fresh parsley, chopped, for garnish*

Directions:

1.   preheat the oven to 425°F.

2.   Place the chicken pieces in a Ziploc bag. Flatten the pieces with a meat tenderizer.

3.   Place the chicken in a bowl and rub the pieces with black pepper and salt.

4.   Add the lemon juice, garlic, oil, and spices and mix well to coat the chicken thoroughly.

5.   Place the onions in an oiled baking dish, then the chicken and tomatoes. Cover the baking dish with aluminum foil.

6.   Bake in the preheated oven for 10 minutes.

7.   After 10 minutes, uncover and bake again for another 8 minutes.

Serving tip: Serve with a sprinkle of parsley over the baked chicken.

Substitution tip: Omit the olive oil and use butter.

Prep
5 m

Portion
4

Cook
15 m

Per Serving
Calories 379; Fat 18g; Sat Fat: 4.8g; Carb 29g; Protein: 29g

MEDITERRANEAN CHICKEN SKILLET WITH MUSHROOMS

- *5-ounce portobello mushrooms, sliced*
- *½ of a large white onion, peeled, cut into round slices*
- *½ tsp. dried thyme*
- *1 ½ tbsp. extra-virgin olive oil, divided*
- *½ tbsp. balsamic vinegar*
- *1 pound chicken breast, cut into strips*
- *¼ tsp. sea salt, divided*
- *¼ tsp. ground black pepper, divided*
- *3 tbsp. white wine*
- *¼ cup vegetable broth*
- *1-ounce Parmesan cheese, sliced*

Directions

1.   Take a large bowl, place chicken strips in it, add salt, black pepper, and thyme, pour in oil, vinegar, and white wine, toss until well coated, and set aside until required.

2.   Take a medium skillet pan, place it over medium heat, add oil, and when hot, add onion and cook for 1 minute until begin to tender.

3.   Add mushroom, salt, and black pepper, pour into the vegetable broth, cook for 5 minutes until softened, and when done, transfer the mushroom mixture into a bowl.

4.   Then add marinated chicken into the pan, cook for 5 minutes, return the mushroom mixture into the pan, and cook for 3 minutes until thoroughly hot.

5.   When done, place the cooked mushroom chicken into a serving plate, place Parmesan slices on the side, and serve.

Prep
10 m

Portion
4

Cook
15 m

Per Serving
Calories: 225; Total fat: 9g; Saturated fat: 1g; Carb: 9g; Protein: 26g; Sodium: 864g; Fiber: 0g

SKIMMED CHICKEN AND ARTICHOKES WITH LEMON

- *4 boneless chicken breast halves, skinless*
- *1/4 tsp. Sea salt*
- *1/4 tsp. freshly ground black pepper*
- *2 tbsp. avocado oil*
- *1 tbsp. lemon juice*
- *2 tbsp. dried crushed oregano*
- *1/4 cup Kalamata olives, pitted and halved*
- *2/3 cup low-sodium chicken broth*
- *14 ounces canned artichoke hearts, packed in water, quartered*

Directions:

1.   Season the chicken breasts with salt and pepper. Add the oil to a large skillet over medium-high heat. When the oil is nice and hot, brown the chicken on both sides - about 2-4 minutes per side.

2.   When the chicken is nicely browned, stir in the lemon juice, oregano, olives, chicken broth, and artichoke hearts. When the broth begins to boil, reduce the heat and simmer with a lid on the pan for 4-5 minutes, or until the chicken is well cooked.

3.   Serve hot.

Substitution tip: You can replace the lemon juice with orange juice.

Prep
10 m

Portion
2

Cook
15 m

Per Serving
Calories: 213 calories; Fat: 8.4 g; Sat. Fat: 1.5 g; Carb: 9.3 g; Protein: 26.1 g; Fiber: 3.2 g

CHICKEN WITH SICILIAN OLIVE

- *2 chicken cutlets, each about 4-ounce*
- *¼ tsp. crushed red pepper*
- *7-ounce cherry tomatoes halved*
- *½ tbsp. capers, rinsed*
- *¼ cup Sicilian olive halves*
- *¼ tsp. ground black pepper*
- *¾ cup chopped spinach, thawed if frozen*
- *½ tbsp. extra-virgin olive oil*

Directions

1.   Take a large bowl, place tomatoes, olives, spinach, capers in it, add red pepper, and stir until well mixed.

2.   Place the chicken cutlets on a cutting board, and then season with black pepper until coated.

3.   Take a medium skillet pan, place it over medium-high heat, add oil, and when hot, add the prepared chicken cutlets and then cook for 4 to 5 minutes per side until nicely brown.

4.   Add the prepared tomato mixture to the pan, switch heat to medium level, cover the pan with its lid and then cook for 5 minutes until the chicken has thoroughly cooked.

5.   When done, place the chicken on a serving plate, add the tomato mixture on the side, and serve.

Ingredient tip: *You can add black olive to add more taste.*

Prep	Portion	Cook	Per Serving
20 m	4	1h 15m	Calories: 611; Fat: 19.8g; Sat fat: 4.8g; Carb: 74.4g; Protein: 45.8g

ARTICHOKES IN BRAISED CHICKEN

- 4 quarters of chicken thigh
- 1 tbsp. olive oil
- 1 yellow onion, chopped
- 1 tsp. salt
- ½ tsp. red pepper flakes, crushed
- 10 canned artichoke hearts, drained and halved
- 8 sprigs fresh thyme
- 1 (16-ounce) can low-sodium butter bean, rinsed and drained
- 4 garlic cloves, minced
- 1 tbsp. black pepper
- 4 cups low-sodium chicken broth
- 2 cups cherry peppers
- 4 tbsp. fresh lemon juice

Directions:

1. Preheat oven to 375degreesF.
2. In a heavy, oven-proof wok set over high heat; heat the oil and sear the chicken for about 5 minutes per side.
3. Place the chicken on a warm plate.
4. In the same wok, add the garlic, onion, salt, black pepper, and red pepper flakes and sauté for about 1 minute.
5. Add the broth and let it come to a boil.
6. Remove the wok from the heat and stir in the cooked chicken, cherry peppers, artichoke hearts, thyme sprigs, and lemon juice.
7. Cover the pan and transfer to the oven.
8. Bake for about 1 hour and then add the beans. Stir to combine.
9. Divide the chicken leg quarters among the serving bowls and top with the artichoke mixture.
10. Serve immediately.

Ingredient tip: Serve alongside a veggie soup.
Substitution tip: chicken wings can also be used.

PREP	Makes	Cook	Per Serving
10 m	20	25 m	Calories 283; Fat 12g; Sodium 232mg; Carb 30g; Fiber 12g; Sugar 4.3g; Protein 12g

MEDITERRANEAN TURKEY MEATBALLS

- 1 yellow onion, diced
- 14 ounces artichoke hearts, diced
- 1 pound ground turkey
- 1 tsp. dried parsley
- 1 tsp. extra-virgin olive oil
- 4 tbsp. basil, chopped
- Sea Salt and pepper, to taste

Directions:

1. Preheat oven to 350 degrees F. Grease a baking sheet.
2. Place the artichokes in a skillet, add the oil and sauté with the diced onions over medium heat for 5 minutes or until the onions are soft.
3. Meanwhile, mix the parsley, basil, and ground turkey with your hands in a large bowl—season to taste.
4. Once the onion mixture has cooled, add it to the bowl and mix thoroughly.
5. Using an ice cream scoop, mix the ground turkey mixture and form into balls.
6. Place the balls on the prepared baking sheet and bake until cooked (about 17 minutes).
7. Serve and enjoy.

Serving tip: Serve over hot rice.
Substitution Tip: Substitute turkey for the chicken.

Prep	Portion	Cook	Per Serving
10 m	4	15 m	Calories: 206; Total fat: 14g; Carb: 1g; Protein: 20g; Sodium: 213mg;

YELLOW CRISPY CHICKEN MEATBALLS

- 1/3 tsp. freshly ground black pepper
- 1/4 tsp. Kosher salt
- 1/2 tsp. turmeric powder
- 1 tsp. ground ginger
- 1 tsp. crushed garlic
- 1/4 cup shallots, finely chopped
- 1 lb. ground chicken
- 1 tbsp. avocado oil (more if needed)

Directions:

Add the pepper, salt, turmeric, ginger, garlic, scallions, and chicken to a large bowl and mix until all ingredients are well combined. Form the chicken into 8 patties about the same size.

2. In a large skillet over medium heat, heat 1 tbsp. avocado oil. When the oil is hot, fry the patties in batches. Fry for 2-3 minutes per side until patties are nicely browned on both sides. Add extra oil to the pan if needed between batches.

3. Serve the meatballs warm on sandwiches of your choice.

Ingredient Tip: You can add some mayonnaise to add more taste.

Prep

1h 10 m

Portion

2

Cook

15 m

Per Serving

Calories: 230.2 calories; Fat: 19.7 g; Sat. Fat: 4.1 g; Carb: 2.1 g; Protein: 11 g; Fiber: 0.4 g

SEASONED GRILLED CHICKEN WINGS

- *1 pound of chicken wings*
- *¼ tsp. turmeric powder*
- *½ of a small white onion, peeled and cut into quarters*
- *¼ tsp. salt*
- *¼ tsp. nutmeg powder*
- *2 garlic cloves, peeled*
- *¼ tsp. red pepper flakes*
- *¼ tsp. cumin powder*
- *1 large lemon, cut in half*
- *¼ tsp. ground coriander*
- *¼ tsp. sweet paprika*
- *2 tsp. lemon juice*
- *3 tbsp. extra-virgin olive oil*

Directions

1. Place in a food processor, add the onion, garlic, lemon juice, oil, cumin, cilantro, paprika, nutmeg, and turmeric, and pulse until combined.

2. Take a large bowl, place the chicken wings in it, season with salt, add the blended onion mixture and toss until well coated.

3. Cover the bowl with its lid, place it in the refrigerator and let it sit for 1 hour, turning it halfway through.

4. When you're ready to cook, take a frying pan, grease it with oil, place it over medium-high heat and let it preheat.

5. Transfer the chicken wings to the skillet and cook for 15 minutes until fully cooked, turning every 5 minutes.

6. Place the cut lemon halves down on the griddle pan and grill until lightly charred.

7. When done, transfer chicken wings to a serving platter, squeeze grilled lemon over the top, and serve.

Ingredient tip: You can replace turmeric powder with ginger powder.

Prep

10 m

Portion

6

Cook

3-4 h

Per Serving

Calories: 475; Total fat: 11g; Saturated fat: 3g; Carb: 48g; Protein: 44g;

HERBED CHICKEN AND SWEET POTATO BAKE

- *1 tbsp. extra virgin olive oil*
- *1/2 cup shallots, chopped*
- *3 tbsp. crushed garlic*
- *6 halves boneless chicken breast, skinless*
- *1 tsp. dried oregano*
- *2 tbsp. lemon zest, finely grated*
- *1 tbsp. quick-cooking tapioca*
- *3 tbsp. sun-dried tomatoes, chopped*
- *1/4 cup Kalamata olives, pitted and chopped*
- *2 1/2 cups chicken broth (divided)*
- *1 3/4 cups uncooked couscous*
- *1/2 cup crumbled feta cheese*

Directions:

1. Heat 1 tbsp. oil in a small skillet over medium heat before adding the scallions, and fry for 3 minutes, or until the scallions turn translucent. Add the garlic and fry for another minute.

2. Scrape the cooked scallions and garlic into a large saucepan over low heat, along with the chicken, oregano, zest, tapioca, tomatoes, olives, and 3/4 cup chicken broth. With the stove on low, cook the chicken for 3-4 hours, or until well done. Shred the chicken, if desired, or cut it into cubes. The chicken can also be left whole.

3. Bring the remaining broth and olive oil to a boil in a large pot over medium heat. Transfer the pot to a wooden cutting board and stir in the uncooked couscous. Let the couscous rest for about 5 minutes, or until all the liquid has been absorbed.

4. Serve the cooked chicken on a bed of couscous, topped with the feta cheese

Substitution tip: You can replace feta cheese with goat cheese.

Fish & Seafood

SPICY GARLIC SALMON

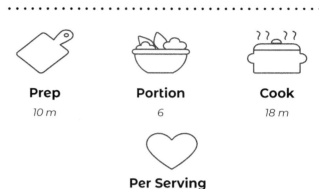

Prep	Portion	Cook
10 m	6	18 m

Per Serving

Calories 306; Fat 18g; Sat Fat: 3.2g; Carb 3g; Protein: 32g

Ingredients:
- 2 pounds of salmon fillet
- 2 tbsp chopped parsley for garnish
- 1/2 tbsp extra-virgin olive oil
- Kosher salt, to taste
- ½ lemon, sliced, for garnish
- Lemon-garlic sauce:
- Zest of one lemon
- 3 tbsp extra virgin olive oil
- 3 tbsp lemon juice
- 5 cloves of garlic, minced
- 1 tsp sweet paprika
- ½ tsp dried oregano
- ½ tsp black pepper

Directions:
1. Preheat the oven to 375°F.
2. Whisk olive oil, pepper, garlic, lemon zest, juice, oregano, and paprika in a bowl and set aside. The garlic and lemon sauce are ready!
3. Line a baking sheet with aluminum foil and brush it with oil.
4. Salt the salmon and arrange it on the baking sheet. Pour the lemon-garlic sauce over the salmon.
5. Bake in the preheated oven for 20 minutes.
6. Bake the salmon for 3 minutes and serve.

Serving tip: Serve garnished with fresh parsley and lemon slices.

Substitution tip: you can replace the evo oil in the garlic and lemon sauce with butter.

Prep	Portion	Cook	Per Serving
10 m	4	8 m	Calories 285; Fat17g; Sat Fat: 3.2g; Carb 4g; Protein: 28g

GRILLED SWORDFISH

- 10 cloves of garlic
- 2 tbsp of lemon juice
- ⅓ of a cup of extra virgin olive oil
- 1 tbsp Spanish paprika
- ¾ tsp cumin
- ¾ tsp salt
- 4 swordfish steaks
- ½ tsp black pepper
- Crushed red pepper to taste
- 2 tsp chopped fresh parsley for garnish.

Directions:

1. Blend the olive oil, pepper, garlic, salt, cumin, paprika, and lemon juice in a blender to make a smooth mixture.
2. Coat the swordfish with the blended mixture and set aside for 15 minutes.
3. Heat a frying pan with a bit of oil over high heat. Add the fish and cook for five minutes on each side.
4. Sprinkle with lemon juice and crushed red pepper, and serve.

Serving tip: Garnish with chopped parsley.

Substitution Tip: Use red pepper for spicier steaks.

Prep	Portion	Cook	Per Serving
5 m	4	20 m	Calories 388; Fat 29g; Sat Fat: 4.6g; Carb 12g; Protein: 21g

HALIBUT FILLETS WITH CINNAMON

- 1/4 cup extra virgin avocado oil
- 3/4 tsp ground cumin
- 1/2 tsp white pepper (divided)
- 1/2 tsp kosher salt (divided)
- 1/2 tsp ground cinnamon
- 1 1/2 tbsp capers, drained
- 15 oz. diced canned tomatoes, drained
- 4 halibut fillets

Directions:

1. Place oil in a large skillet over medium heat. When oil is hot, add cumin and sauté for about 1 minute, or until fragrant. Add 1/4 tsp pepper, 1/4 tsp salt, cinnamon, capers, and canned tomatoes. Stir-fry sauce for about 10 minutes or until thickened.
2. Pat the fish dry with paper towels. Season the fillets on both sides with the remaining salt and pepper. Lay the seasoned fillets in the sauce over low heat and cover the pan. Allow the fish to simmer for 8-10 minutes, or until opaque and flakes easily.
3. Plate the fish and serve immediately, with the sauce poured over the cooked fish. Enjoy!

Prep	Portion	Cook	Per Serving
10 m	2	30 m	Calories 430; Fat 29g; Sat Fat: 3.9g; Carb 25g; Protein: 23g

SHRIMP SALAD WITH AVOCADO

- 1/2 pound medium cooked shrimp
- Freshly ground black pepper
- ½ tsp sea salt
- 1/4 tsp. cayenne pepper
- 1 tbsp. mayonnaise
- 1 tbsp. freshly squeezed lemon juice
- 1 spring onion, thinly sliced
- 1 large Hass avocado, peeled, pitted, and diced
- 4 cups arugula
- 2 tbsp. balsamic vinegar
- 1 tbsp. extra virgin olive oil
- 1/2 cup cherry tomatoes, halved
- 1/4 cup shelled pistachios, coarsely chopped

Directions:

1. Remove shrimp tails and discard them. Cut each shrimp into 3 sections before placing them in a large bowl. Season the shrimp with a few grinds of pepper and 1/8 tsp. salt. Add the cayenne pepper, mayonnaise, lemon juice, and spring onions, stirring until all ingredients are well combined. Stir in avocado until just combined. Do not overmix.
2. Place the arugula in a large salad bowl and toss with vinegar and olive oil—season to taste with salt and pepper.
3. Serve the shrimp on the bed of dressed arugula garnished with chopped pistachios and tomatoes.

Prep
5 m

Portion
4

Cook
15 m

Per Serving
Calories: 303; Total fat: 16g; Saturated fat; 3g: Carb: 9g; Protein: 30g; Sodium: 510mg; Fiber: 2g

SALMON FILLET WITH SWEET CHILI SAUCE

- 2 tbsp. sweet chili sauce (divided)
- 1 spring onion, finely chopped
- 1 cucumber, finely chopped
- 1 cup fresh blackberries
- 1 tbsp. avocado oil
- 4 salmon fillets with skin on
- 1/2 tsp. flaked sea salt
- 1/2 tsp. freshly ground black pepper

Directions:

1. In a medium-sized bowl, gently stir together 1 tbsp. sweet chili sauce and the spring onion, cucumber, and blackberries. Set aside.

2. Brush a grill with 1 tbsp. avocado oil and preheat to medium-high. Season the salmon fillets with salt and pepper before placing them skin side down on the heated grill. Place a lid on the grill and cook the fillets for 2-3 minutes before brushing them with the remaining chili sauce. Replace the lid and continue to cook for 10-12 minutes, or until the fillets are opaque.

3. Serve the cooked salmon warm, topped with the blackberry mixture.

Ingredient tip: Add some lemon zest to add more flavor.

Prep
10 m

Portion
4

Cook
15 m

Per Serving
Calories 228; Fat 10g; Sodium 284mg; Carb 9g; Fiber 2g; Sugar 2g; Protein 28g

HALIBUT WITH KALE

- 3 tbsp. extra-virgin olive oil, divided
- 3 cups cabbage, coarsely chopped
- 2 cups cherry tomatoes, halved
- 4 (4-ounce) boneless, skinless halibut fillets
- Juice and zest of 1 lemon
- Sea salt and black pepper, to taste
- 1 tbsp. fresh basil, chopped

Directions:

1. Preheat oven to 375degreesF.

2. Lightly grease an 8-inch x 8-inch baking dish with 2 tsp. olive oil.

3. Arrange the cabbage in the bottom of the baking dish and top with the cherry tomatoes and halibut.

4. Pour in the remaining olive oil, lemon juice, lemon zest, basil, salt, and pepper.

5. Cook until the fish flakes easily and the vegetables are wilted (about 15 minutes).

6. Serve and enjoy. Garnish with cilantro.

Suggestion Tip: You can also cook the fish and vegetables in individual foil packets on a baking sheet instead of in a pan for easy serving.

Prep
5 m

Portion
2

Cook
10 m

Per Serving
Calories 324; Fat 27g; Sat Fat: 3.5g; Carb 10g; Protein: 28g

COCONUT MARINATED SALMON

- 2 medium scallions, sliced
- 1 tbsp sesame seeds
- 1/2 tsp cayenne pepper
- 1 tbsp toasted sesame oil
- 2 tbsp extra virgin olive oil (plus 2 tbsp)
- 1 tbsp coconut amino
- 8 oz. of wild sushi salmon, cut into small cubes
- 1/2 medium cauliflower
- 2 tbsp. avocado oil
- 1 tbsp freshly squeezed lemon juice
- ½ tsp Kosher salt
- White pepper
- 1 medium English cucumber, diced
- 1 large avocado, cut into cubes
- 1/2 sheet of nori, cut into small pieces

Directions:

1. In a medium bowl, whisk together the shallots, sesame seeds, cayenne pepper, toasted sesame oil, 2 tbsp olive oil, and coconut amino. Add the salmon cubes and stir to coat. Set aside on the counter while you prepare the rest of the dish.

2. Break the cauliflower into florets and blend on high speed until the pieces resemble rice. Heat the avocado oil in a large skillet over medium heat. Add the cauliflower rice when the oil is hot and saute for 5 to 7 minutes. Transfer the skillet to a wooden cutting board and add the lemon juice—season with salt and pepper.

3. Divide the cooked cauliflower rice between 2 bowls and top with the marinated salmon. Garnish with the cucumber and avocado before sprinkling with the remaining olive oil and nori pieces. Serve immediately.

Prep

10 m

Portion

4

Cook

10 m

Per Serving

Calories 159; Fat 6.7; Sodium 989mg; Carb 5.4g; Fiber 0.4g; Sugar 3.1g; Protein 20.5g

CRAB PATTIES

- 2 eggs, lightly beaten
- 18 ounces can crab meat, drained
- 2 ½ tbsp. mayonnaise
- ¼ cup almond flour
- 1 tsp. dried parsley
- 1 tsp. Italian seasoning
- 1 ½ tbsp. Dijon mustard
- Pepper
- Sea salt

Directions:

1. Add crab meat and remaining ingredients into the bowl and mix well.

2. Make patties from crab mixture and place them into the air fryer basket.

3. Cook at 320degrees F for 10 minutes. Turn patties halfway through. Serve with your favorite dip.

Ingredient Tip: Add 1 tsp. of dill.

Prep

5 m

Portion

2

Cook

25 m

Per Serving

Calories: 227 calories; Fat: 11.7 g; Sat. Fat: 1.7 g; Carb: 4.5 g; Protein: 26.2 g; Fiber: 1.3 g

BAKED COD WITH TOMATOES

- 1 cup of cherry tomatoes.
- 2 large pieces of cod fillets
- 2 tbsp. basil leaves, torn into pieces
- ½ medium shallot, sliced
- 2 tsp. minced garlic
- ¼ tsp. salt, divided
- 1 tsp. lemon zest
- ¼ tsp. ground black pepper, divided
- ¼ tsp. red chili pepper flakes
- 1 tsp. red wine vinegar
- 3 tsp. extra-virgin olive oil

Directions

1. Turn on the oven, set it to 218 degrees C or 425 degrees F, and preheat it.

2. Meanwhile, take a medium baking dish, add the shallots, cherry tomato, garlic, salt, oil, black pepper, and red wine vinegar and stir until combined.

3. Place the dish in the oven, bake the mixture for 10 minutes, stir until combined, and set aside.

4. In the meantime, arrange the cod fillets on a cutting board, drizzle with the oil and then season with salt, black pepper, and chili pepper until coated.

5. When the shallot mixture is cooked, remove it from the oven, change the heat to 205 degrees C or 400 degrees F, and let it preheat.

6. Place the cod fillets in the baking dish with the roasted tomatoes in between and continue cooking for 10 minutes.

7. Then shake the pan to move the tomatoes, add the lemon zest, and cook for another 4 minutes.

8. When done, toss the basil leaves with the roasted tomatoes, arrange the cod fillets on a serving platter, with the tomatoes on the side, and serve.

Prep

10 m

Portion

4

Cook

8 m

Per Serving

Calories 526; Fat 34g; Sat Fat: 5.2g; Carb 17g; Protein: 39g

HALIBUT WITH LEMON AND BASIL

- 24 ounces of halibut fillets
- 2 cloves of garlic, crushed
- 2 tbsp extra-virgin olive oil
- 2 tsp drained capers
- 3 tbsp fresh basil, sliced
- 2 1/2 tbsp fresh lemon juice

Directions:

1. Mix garlic, lemon juice, olive oil, 2 tbsp basil, pepper, and salt in a small bowl.

2. Preheat grill to medium-high heat.

3. Season fish fillets with pepper and salt and brush with garlic.

4. Place the fish fillets on the grill and cook for 4 minutes on each side.

Serving tip: Transfer the fish fillets to a serving platter and top with the garlic mixture and remaining basil.

Substitution tip: Add seasonings of your choice.

Prep
15 m

Portion
4

Cook
40 m

Per Serving
Calories 331; Fat 21g; Sat Fat: 3.2g; Carb 14g; Protein: 21g

HALIBUT PARCEL WITH OLIVES AND CAPERS

- 1 large tomato, chopped
- 1 onion, chopped
- 1 can of pitted Kalamata olives (5 ounces)
- ¼ cup extra-virgin olive oil
- Sea salt and black pepper, to taste
- 1 tbsp of Greek seasoning
- ¼ cup capers
- 1 tbsp fresh lemon juice
- 4 halibut fillets (6 ounces)

Directions:

1. Preheat the oven to 350°F.
2. Mix a bowl of tomato, onion, olives, capers, oil, lemon juice, salt, and black pepper.
3. Season the halibut fillets evenly with the Greek dressing.
4. Arrange the halibut fillets on a large aluminum foil and cover them with the tomato mixture.
5. Carefully fold over all edges to create a large parcel.
6. Place the parcel on a baking sheet and bake for about 40 minutes.
7. Remove from oven and serve hot.

Serving tip: Serve with sautéed vegetables.

Substitution tip: You can also add jalapeños.

Prep
5 m

Portion
6

Cook
30 m

Per Serving
Calories 372; Fat 25g; Sat Fat: 6g; Carb 27g; Protein: 11g

MEDITERRANEAN-STYLE SQUID TUBES

- 1/2 cup, plus 4 tbsp, of extra virgin olive oil (divided)
- 2 medium shallots, finely chopped
- 1 cup raisins
- 6 cups panko breadcrumbs
- 3/4 cup fresh parsley, finely chopped (divided)
- 1 1/4 cups grated Parmesan cheese (divided)
- 4 tbsp crushed garlic in oil
- 12 large tubes of squid, cleaned
- 4 whole garlic cloves, finely chopped
- 28 oz. canned tomatoes, crushed
- 1 tbsp kosher salt
- 1 tsp white pepper
- 1/2 cup fresh basil, finely chopped
- 1 tsp dried oregano, chopped

Directions:

1. Preheat the oven to 350°F, with the rack in the center.
2. In a large skillet over medium-high heat, heat 2 tbsp of oil. When the oil is hot, sauté the shallots for about 5 minutes, or until softened and translucent. Scrape the shallots into a large bowl. Add 1/2 cup olive oil, 1 cup raisins, 6 cups bread crumbs, 1/2 cup parsley, 1 cup Parmesan cheese, and 4 tsp garlic until all ingredients are well combined.
3. Use 1 tbsp of oil to grease the inside of a large casserole dish. Sp spoon some of the breadcrumb mixture into each squid tube using a tsp. Use toothpicks to secure the openings and prevent the filling from spilling out during cooking. Arrange the stuffed tubes in the prepared casserole dish in a single layer. Place the dish in the preheated oven for 10 minutes.
4. Meanwhile, in a large skillet over medium-high heat, heat the remaining 2 tbsp of olive oil. When the oil is hot, sauté the garlic for 30 seconds. Add the tomatoes, salt, pepper, basil, and oregano. Simmer the sauce for 5 minutes, stirring, so the flavors blend.
5. Transfer the casserole to a wooden cutting board and pour the sauce over all the stuffed tubes. Garnish the sauce with the remaining cheese and parsley before returning the casserole to the oven and baking for another 10 minutes. Serve hot.

Prep	Portion	Cook	Per Serving
10 m	4	30 m	Calories 108; Fat2g; Sat Fat: 0.4g; Carb 3g; Protein: 17g

MEDITERRANEAN COAST-STYLE GRILLED OCTOPUS

- ½ tsp. chopped parsley, fresh
- 1 pound octopus, head and beak removed
- ½ tsp. Sea salt, divided
- ¼ tsp. ground black pepper
- 1 tsp. lemon juice
- ½ tsp. black peppercorns
- 1 tsp. extra virgin olive oil
- 1 capful of white wine

Directions

1. Take a large pot half full of water, put it over high heat, add the salt, peppercorns, and wine cap, and bring the mixture to a boil.

2. Meanwhile, place the octopus on a cutting board and pound it all over with a wooden spoon.

3. When the water begins to boil, add the octopus, turn the heat to medium-low, cover the pot with its lid, and let it cook for 20-30 minutes, or until tender.

4. Then remove the pot from the heat, remove the octopus, and let it cool for 10 minutes at room temperature.

5. Meanwhile, take a grill pan, grease it with 1 tbsp. of oil, place it over medium-high heat and let it preheat.

6. Place the octopus on the skillet, cook it for 4 minutes per side until slightly charred, then transfer it to a cutting board and cut it into pieces.

7. Transfer octopus pieces to a plate, drizzle with oil and lemon juice, sprinkle with salt, black pepper, and parsley, and serve.

Ingredient tip: To obtain a fluffy octopus, you need to buy a frozen one, not fresh.

Prep	Portion	Cook	Per Serving
10 m	4	24 m	Calories: 151; Total fat: 9g; Carb: 1g; Protein: 16g;

GRILLED PLAICE FILLETS WITH GARLIC

- 1/4 tsp. Sea salt
- 1 tsp. freshly ground black pepper
- 1 tsp. crushed garlic
- 1 lemon, zest (reserved segments for garnish)
- 1 tbsp. avocado oil
- 4 flounder fillets, dried
- 1 tbsp. capers, chopped
- 1/4 cup fresh parsley, chopped

Directions:

1. Line a large baking sheet with foil and spray lightly with cooking spray. Set the oven rack to preheat on low, with the wire rack about 6 inches away from the rack.

2. In a small glass bowl, whisk together the salt, pepper, garlic, lemon zest, and avocado oil. Place the flounder fillets on the prepared baking sheet and brush with the oil mixture. Place the baking sheet in the oven for about 10 minutes or until the fish is no longer transparent. Cooking time may vary depending on the thickness of the fillets.

3. Plate the grilled fish and garnish with the capers, parsley, and reserved lemon wedges before serving.

Ingredient tip: Add some black olives to add more flavor.

Prep	Portion	Cook	Per Serving
10 m	2	5 m	Calories 171; Fat 5g; Sat Fat: 2.2g; Carb 4g; Protein: 26g

SHRIMP SALAD

- ½ pound cooked shrimp
- ⅓ cup Greek yogurt
- ½ tsp. lemon juice
- 1 garlic clove, minced
- 2 tbsp. feta cheese, crumbled
- ½ tsp. dill
- pepper
- ½ tsp Sea Salt

Directions:

1. Add shrimp and remaining ingredients to the bowl and mix well.

Serving tip: Garnish with dill and serve.

Substitution tip: Add 1 small chopped onion.

Prep
5 m

Portion
4

Cook
0 m

Per Serving

Calories: 279; Total fat: 13g; Saturated fat: 2g; Carb: 19g; Protein: 22g;
Sodium: 421g; Fiber: 7g

HEALTHY TUNA AND BEAN ROLLS

- *15 ounces canned cannellini beans, drained and rinsed*
- *12 ounces canned light tuna in spring water, drained and flaked*
- *1/8 tsp. white pepper*
- *1/8 tsp. Kosher salt*
- *1 tbsp. fresh parsley, chopped*
- *2 tbsp. extra virgin avocado oil*
- *1/4 cup red onion, chopped*
- *12 romaine lettuce leaves*
- *1 medium-sized ripe Hass avocado, sliced*

Directions:

1.   Mix the beans, tuna, pepper, salt, parsley, avocado oil, and red onion in a large bowl.

2.   Spread some of the mixtures on each lettuce leaf and top with the sliced avocado before folding and serving.

Substitution tip: You can use a different salad with long leaves.

Prep
5 m

Portion
4

Cook
20 m

Per Serving

Calories: 290.8 calories; Fat: 9.8 g; Sat. Fat: 1.6 g; Carb: 36.8 g;
Protein: 13.6 g; Fiber: 1.8 g

SICILIAN-STYLE SPAGHETTI WITH TUNA AND CAPERS

- *1 small white onion, peeled, sliced*
- *½ tbsp. chopped parsley, fresh*
- *1 tbsp. capers, drained*
- *5 ounces canned tuna, drained*
- *½ pound whole-wheat spaghetti*
- *¼ tsp. crushed red flakes*
- *1 tbsp. extra-virgin olive oil*

Directions

1.   Take a medium pot half-full water, place it over medium-high heat, bring it to a boil, add spaghetti and cook for 10 minutes until tender.

2.   When done, take out ½ cup cooking water, set it aside, and drain the spaghetti.

3.   Take a large skillet pan, place it over medium heat, add oil, and when hot, add onion and cook for 5 minutes, or until light brown.

4.   Add tuna, capers, and red pepper, stir until mixed and cook for another minute or thoroughly hot.

5.   Add the cooked spaghetti, stir until combined, pour in the reserved pasta water, and cook for 2 minutes or thoroughly hot.

6.   Sprinkle with parsley and then serve.

Prep
10 m

Portion
4

Cook
0 m

Per Serving

Calories 295; Fat 11g; Sat Fat: 2.2g; Carb 22g; Protein: 31g

TUNA AND COUSCOUS

- *1 cup chicken broth*
- *1¼ cup of couscous*
- *A pinch of salt and black pepper*
- *10 ounces canned tuna, drained and flaked*
- *1 quart of cherry tomatoes, cut in half*
- *½ cup chilies, cut into slices*
- *⅓ cup chopped parsley*
- *1 tbsp extra virgin olive oil*
- *¼ cup capers, drained*
- *½ lemon, squeezed*

Directions:

1.   Place broth in a pot and bring to a boil over medium-high heat.

2.   Add couscous, stir, remove from heat, cover and set aside for 10 minutes. Stir with a fork and transfer to a bowl.

3.   Add the tuna and the rest of the ingredients, stir and serve immediately.

Serving tip: Serve over lettuce and with a garnish of parsley.

Substitution tip: you can substitute couscous with cooked quinoa.

Prep	Portion	Cook	Per Serving
5 m	2	10 m	Calories: 297 calories; Fat: 12.3 g; Sat. Fat: 17.8 g; Carb: 3.1 g; Protein: 43 g; Fiber: 123 g

GRILLED FISH FILLET WITH GENOVESE PESTO SAUCE

- 1 tbsp. pine nuts
- ½ cup basil leaves, fresh
- 2 cloves of garlic
- 2 medium fillets of white fish
- ½ tsp. salt
- ¼ tsp. black pepper
- 1 cup and 1 tbsp. extra-virgin olive oil
- 1 tbsp. grated Parmesan cheese

Directions

1. Switch on the oven, then set it to 400 degrees F and let it preheat.

2. Meanwhile, place the fish fillets on a large plate, drizzle with 1 tbsp. oil, and season with salt and black pepper until coated.

3. Take a baking tray, line it with parchment paper, arrange the fish fillets on it and then bake for 10 minutes until the skin turns crisp.

4. Meanwhile, place basil leaves into a blender, add pine nuts, garlic, Parmesan cheese, 1 cup oil, and pulse until smooth.

5. When done, place the fish fillets on a serving plate, drizzle the prepared pesto sauce on top, and serve.

Prep	Portion	Cook	Per Serving
5 m	4	15 m	Calories 438; Fat 27g; Sat Fat: 5g; Carb 21g; Protein: 30g

PAN-FRIED SWORDFISH

- 4 tbsp extra virgin avocado oil (divided)
- 1 small shallot, thinly sliced
- 2 tbsp crushed garlic
- 1/2 medium eggplant, diced
- 2 medium zucchini, diced
- 1 cup whole Greek olives, pitted
- 2 cups cherry tomatoes, cut in half
- 4 swordfish fillets with skin on, dried
- ½ tsp Kosher salt
- Freshly ground black pepper
- 1/4 cup green olive tapenade with harissa

Directions:

1. Preheat the oven to 375°F, with the rack in the center.

2. Heat 2 tbsp of oil in a large skillet over medium-high heat. When the oil is hot, sauté the shallots and garlic for about 5 minutes, or until the shallots turn translucent. Add the eggplant and sauté until it begins to tender about 3 minutes. Add the zucchini and stir-fry for another 5 minutes until all the vegetables are tender and crispy at the edges. Add the olives and tomatoes and sauté, stirring, for 2 minutes. Set the pan aside, away from the heat.

3. Season the fish generously with salt and pepper. Heat the remaining olive oil in an ovenproof skillet over medium-high heat. When the oil is hot, place the fish fillets skin-side down in the pan and fry for 3 minutes. The edges should start to turn solid. Turn the fish in the skillet before transferring it to the oven and cooking for another 3 minutes. The fish should be completely firm and flaky when ready.

4. Top the cooked swordfish with fried vegetables and olive tapenade. Serve immediately.

Prep	Portion	Cook	Per Serving
10 m	2	20 m	Calories 454; Fat 18g; Sat Fat: 3.7g; Carb 1g; Protein: 66g

PARMESAN SALMON

- 2 salmon fillets
- 2 tbsp grated Parmesan cheese
- 1 tbsp extra-virgin olive oil
- 1 sliced tomato
- 1 tbsp dried basil

Directions:

1. Preheat the oven to 375° F.

2. Arrange fish fillets on a baking sheet. Sprinkle with basil.

3. Arrange tomato slices on top of fish fillets.

4. Drizzle with oil. Sprinkle the salmon with cheese.

5. Bake for 20 minutes.

Serving tip: Garnish with basil and serve.

Substitution tip: Season the salmon fillets with Italian herbs.

Prep	Portion	Cook	Per Serving
10 m	4	1h 15 m	Calories 733; Fat 22.3g; Sodium 1012mg; Carb 44.9g; Fiber 4.9g; Sugar 14.8g; Protein 55g

GREEK-STYLE STUFFED SQUID

- ¼ cup golden raisins
- ¼ cup pine nuts, toasted
- ½ cup red wine
- ½ cup plain dry bread crumbs
- 1 (15-ounce) can of tomato sauce
- 1 clove minced garlic
- 1 tbsp. dried mint
- 16 medium squid bodies, plus 6 ounces of tentacles, chopped
- 2 tbsp. extra-virgin olive oil
- 3 onions, finely chopped
- 4 anchovy fillets, rinsed and chopped
- 5 tbsp. fresh parsley, chopped
- Sea Salt and pepper, to taste

Directions:

1. Heat 1 tbsp. oil in a 12-inch non-stick skillet over moderate-high heat until it begins to shimmer.

2. Place two-thirds of the onions in and cook until tender (about 5 minutes). Add squid tentacles and cook until no longer translucent, 1-2 minutes.

3. Add the pine nuts, mint, and ¼ tsp. pepper and cook until aromatic, about 1 minute.

4. Move the mixture to a large bowl and stir in the bread crumbs, ¼ cup parsley, raisins, and anchovies.

5. Sprinkle with salt and pepper to taste and let cool slightly.

6. Using a small soup spoon, portion 2 tbsp. of stuffing into each squid's body, gently pressing down on the stuffing to create a 1-inch gap at the top.

7. Thread a toothpick through the opening of each squid to close securely.

8. Heat the remaining 1 tbsp. oil in the now-empty skillet over moderate to high heat until it begins to shimmer.

9. Place the remaining onions and cook until tender (about 5 minutes).

10. Stir in the garlic, ¼ tsp. salt, and ¼ tsp. pepper and cook until aromatic, about half a minute.

11. Stir in the wine, tomato sauce, salt, and pepper, and bring to a boil.

12. Add the squid to the sauce.

13. Reduce the heat to low, cover, and simmer gently until the sauce has thickened slightly and the squid pierces easily with a paring knife, about 1 hour, turning the squid halfway through cooking.

14. Season the sauce with salt and pepper to taste.

15. Remove toothpicks from squid and garnish with 1 tbsp. parsley.

16. Serve. Garnish with basil leaves.

Substitution tip: Add red pepper to add more flavor.

Prep	Portion	Cook	Per Serving
5 m	4	10 m	Calories: 198 calories; Fat: 5 g; Sat. Fat: 1 g; Carb: 2 g; Protein: 35 g;

BAKED HALIBUT

- ½ pound of halibut
- ¼ tbsp. sesame seeds
- ¼ tbsp. dried oregano
- ¼ tsp. crushed red pepper
- ¼ tsp. ground cumin
- ¼ tsp. salt
- 1 tbsp. extra-virgin olive oil
- 1 tsp. lemon juice

Directions

1. Turn on the oven, set it to 218 degrees C or 425 degrees F, and let it preheat.

2. Meanwhile, take a baking sheet, line it with baking paper, and set it aside until needed.

3. Take a small bowl, place the salt, cumin, red pepper, oregano, and sesame seeds in it, and mix until combined.

4. Place the halibut in a shallow dish, brush with the oil, season with the prepared salt mixture and transfer to the prepared baking dish.

5. Place the prepared baking dish with the halibut in the oven and bake for 10 minutes or until flaky.

6. Serve immediately.

Prep	Portion	Cook	Per Serving
10 m	4	30 m	Calories: 256 calories; Fat: 5.9 g; Sat. Fat: 1.06 g; Carb: 7.1 g; Protein: 41.2 g

ITALIAN-STYLE GRILLED OCTOPUS

- ½ tsp. chopped parsley, fresh
- 1 pound octopus, head and beak removed
- ½ tsp. salt, divided
- ¼ tsp. ground black pepper
- 1 tsp. lemon juice
- ½ tsp. black peppercorns
- 1 tsp. extra-virgin olive oil
- 1 cupful of wine

Directions

1. Take a large pot half full of water, put it over high heat, add the salt, peppercorns, and wine cap, and bring the mixture to a boil.

2. Meanwhile, place the octopus on a cutting board and pound it all over with a wooden spoon.

3. When the water begins to boil, add the octopus, turn the heat to medium-low, cover the pot with its lid, and let it cook for 20-30 minutes, or until tender.

4. Then remove the pot from the heat, remove the octopus, and let it cool for 10 minutes at room temperature.

5. Meanwhile, take a grill pan, grease it with 1 tbsp. of oil, place it over medium-high heat and let it preheat.

6. Place the octopus on the skillet, cook it for 4 minutes per side until slightly charred, then transfer it to a cutting board and cut it into pieces.

7. Transfer octopus pieces to a plate, drizzle with oil and lemon juice, sprinkle with salt, black pepper, and parsley, and serve.

Ingredient tip: To obtain a fluffy octopus, you need to buy a frozen one, not fresh.

Prep	Portion	Cook	Per Serving
15 m	4	15 m	Calories: 151; Fat: 5.8g; Sat fat: 3.3g; Carb: 3.8g; Fiber: 0.8g; Sugar: 0.3g; Protein: 22.2g

TILAPIA WITH CAPERS

- 1½ tsp. paprika
- 1½ tsp. ground cumin
- 2 shallots, finely chopped
- 2 tbsp. fresh lemon juice
- 1 pound tilapia, cut into 8 pieces
- Salt and black pepper, to taste
- 3 garlic cloves, minced
- 1½ tbsp. unsalted butter, melted
- ¼ cup capers

Directions:

1. Preheat the oven to 375degreesF and line a baking sheet with baking paper.

2. Combine the paprika, cumin, salt, and black pepper in a small bowl and mix well.

3. Combine the butter, garlic, scallions, and lemon juice in another small bowl and mix well.

4. Sprinkle the tilapia fillets evenly with the spice mixture and coat generously with the butter mixture.

5. Arrange the tilapia fillets in a single layer on the baking sheet and top with the capers.

6. Bake for about 15 minutes and serve hot.

Serving tip: Serve on a bed of basmati rice.

Ingredient Tip: Tilapia can be substituted with halibut.

Prep	Portion	Cook	Per Serving
10 m	4	15 m	Calories 216; Fat 11g; Sat Fat: 1.7g; Carb 18g; Protein: 11g

HALIBUT IN HERB CRUST

- ⅓ cup fresh parsley
- ¼ cup fresh dill
- ¼ cup fresh chives
- 1 tsp of lemon zest
- ¾ cup panko breadcrumbs
- 1 tbsp extra virgin olive oil
- ¼ tsp freshly ground black pepper
- ½ tsp sea salt
- 4-6 ounces of halibut fillets

Directions:

1. Chop fresh dill, chives, and parsley.

2. Line a baking sheet with aluminum foil. Set the oven to 400°F.

3. In a bowl, combine salt, pepper, lemon zest, olive oil, chives, dill, parsley, and bread crumbs.

4. Rinse the halibut thoroughly. Use paper towels to dry it before baking. Arrange the fish on the baking sheet.

5. Spread crumbs over the fish and press onto each fillet.

6. Bake until the top is golden brown and easily flaky (about 10-15 minutes).

Serving tip: :Serve with salted potatoes and peas.

Substitution tip: You can use other fresh herbs of your liking.

Snack & Appetizers

ZUCCHINI FRITTERS

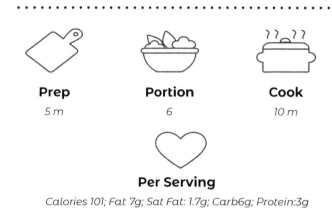

Prep
5 m

Portion
6

Cook
10 m

Per Serving

Calories 101; Fat 7g; Sat Fat: 1.7g; Carb6g; Protein:3g

Ingredients:

- 2 zucchini, peeled and grated
- 1 cup fresh parsley, chopped
- ½ tsp. fine sea salt
- ½ tsp. black pepper
- 1 sweet onion, finely chopped
- 2 garlic cloves, minced
- ½ tsp. ground allspice
- 2 tbsp. extra virgin olive oil
- 4 large eggs

Directions:

1. Line a plate with paper towels and set it aside.
2. Mix the onion, parsley, garlic, zucchini, pepper, allspice, and sea salt in a large bowl.
3. In another bowl, beat the eggs before adding them to the zucchini mixture. Make sure it is mixed well.
4. Place a large skillet over medium heat.
5. Heat the olive oil and then pour ¼ cup of the mixture into the skillet to create the pancakes.
6. Cook for three minutes or until the bottom settles.
7. Flip and cook for another three minutes.
8. Transfer pancakes to a lined plate so they can drain.
9. Serve.

Ingredient Tip: Serve with pita bread.

Substitution tip: You can substitute eggs for a dairy-free option.

Prep	Portion	Cook	Per Serving
15 m + 2h Cooling	10	0 m	Calories 104; Fat 1g; Sat Fat: 0g; Carb20g; Protein:4g

GAZPACHO OF CHICKPEAS AND VEGETABLES

- 1 large fresh tomato, chopped
- 1 can of low-sodium chickpeas, rinsed and drained
- 1 large cucumber, peeled, seeded and finely chopped
- ½ yellow bell pepper, seeded and chopped
- 2 tbsp sweet onion, finely chopped
- 1 large garlic clove, chopped
- 1 can (46 fluid ounces) of low-sodium tomato juice
- A pinch of chili sauce
- ½ cup fresh parsley, chopped
- 1 stalk of celery, finely chopped
- ½ red bell pepper, seeded and chopped
- 2 shallots, chopped
- ¼ cup fresh parsley, chopped
- 1 tbsp fresh lemon juice
- 1 tsp curry powder
- Black pepper, to taste

Directions:

1. Place all ingredients except parsley in a large bowl and mix thoroughly.
2. Cover the bowl tightly with plastic wrap and place it in the refrigerator.
3. Chill for about 2 hours and serve garnished with parsley.

Serving tip: Serve with a sprinkling of oregano.

Substitution tip: More vegetables can be added.

Prep	Portion	Cook	Per Serving
10 m	2	10 m	Calories: 138 calories; Fat: 9.4 g; Sat. Fat: 2 g; Carb: 13.8 g; Protein: 2.4 g; Fiber: 4 g

EGGPLANT DIP

- 1 small eggplant
- 1 small tomato, diced
- 4 tbsp. diced cucumber
- ½ cup parsley leaves
- ½ tsp. chopped garlic
- ¼ tsp. salt, divided
- ¼ tsp. ground black pepper, divided
- ½ tsp. lemon pepper seasoning
- ¼ tsp. Aleppo pepper
- 1 tbsp. tahini paste
- 1 tbsp. extra-virgin olive oil
- ¾ tbsp. yogurt, low-fat, unsweetened
- ½ tbsp. lemon juice, divided

Directions

1. Turn the stove on medium heat, place the eggplant on the burner, and then cook for 8 to 10 minutes until charred, rotate occasionally.
2. When done, transfer the eggplant to a plate, let it cool, and then peel it.
3. Place the peeled eggplant on a drainer, let it rest for 3 minutes to drain any liquid, and then place in a food processor.
4. Add garlic, tahini, yogurt, lemon juice, salt, black pepper, lemon pepper seasoning, and Aleppo pepper, and then pulse for 1 minute until smooth.
5. Spoon the prepared dip into a serving bowl, cover the bowl with its lid, place in a refrigerator and let it rest for 30 minutes.
6. Meanwhile, take a medium bowl, add tomato, cucumber, parsley, salt, and black pepper, drizzle with oil and lemon juice, and stir until well mixed.
7. After 30 minutes, let the eggplant dip rest at room temperature for 10 minutes, top with the prepared tomato mixture, and then serve with crackers.

Prep	Portion	Cook	Per Serving
15 m	4	10 m	Calories: 200; Fat: 11.4g; Sat fat: 5.3g; Carb: 12.3g; Fiber: 2.4g; Sugar: 1.9g; Protein: 14.1g

CHICKEN AND CHEESE WHITE PIZZA

- 1 tbsp. Greek vinaigrette
- 2 flat-breads
- ½ cup feta cheese, crumbled
- ½ cup artichoke hearts packed in water, rinsed, drained, and chopped
- ½ cup chicken breast cooked in strips, chopped
- ⅛ tsp. dried oregano, crushed
- 1 cup part-skim mozzarella cheese, shredded
- ¼ cup Parmesan cheese, grated
- ½ cup black olives, pitted and sliced
- ⅛ tsp. dried basil, crushed
- Pinch of black pepper

Directions:

1. Preheat oven to 390degreesF.
2. Arrange the buns on a large baking sheet and glaze each with the vinaigrette.
3. Place feta cheese on each bun, followed by the vegetables, Parmesan cheese, and chicken.
4. Sprinkle with black pepper and dried herbs.
5. Top each bread evenly with the mozzarella cheese.
6. Bake for 10 minutes until cheese is melted.
7. Remove from oven and set aside for about 2 minutes.
8. Slice each flat-bread into two pieces and serve. Serve with your favorite sauce.

Substitution Tip: Black olives can be replaced with green olives.

Prep	Portion	Cook	Per Serving
10 m	2 Cups	10 m	Calories 35; Fat 2g; Sat Fat: 1g; Carb 2g; Protein: 1g

ROASTED ALMONDS

- 1 tbsp extra virgin olive oil
- 1 tsp salt
- 2 cups whole, peeled, raw almonds

Directions:

1. Heat the oil in a 12-inch nonstick skillet over moderate or high heat until it shatters.
2. Put in the almonds, salt, and pepper and reduce the heat to moderate-low.
3. Cook, often stirring, until almonds become aromatic and their color becomes a little deep, about 8 minutes.
4. Transfer the almonds to a paper towel-lined plate and let them cool before serving.

Serving tip: Serve over ice cream.

Substitution tip: Add chili pepper for a spicier result.

Prep	Portion	Cook	Per Serving
5 m	4	2 m	Calories 90; Fat 3g; Sat Fat: 1g; Carb 9g; Protein: 6g

EGGS AND HAM

- 1/8 tsp white pepper
- 1/8 tsp smoked sweet paprika
- 1 large egg
- White of 2 large eggs
- 2 tbsp mozzarella cheese, grated
- 1 spring onion, chopped
- 1 slice ham, chopped
- 2 whole-wheat pita pocket halves

Directions:

1. Place the pepper, paprika, egg and egg whites in a medium-sized glass bowl. Whisk until eggs are light and frothy. Add the cheese, spring onions and ham, stirring gently to combine.
2. Place the bowl in the microwave for about 1 minute before stirring and microwaving for another 30 to 60 seconds, or until the eggs are well cooked.
3. Spread the cooked eggs and ham into the pita halves and serve.

Prep	Makes	Cook	Per Serving
10 m	22	10 m	Calories 54; Fat 2g; Sodium 32mg; Carb 9g; Fiber 1.9g; Sugar 5.5g; Protein 1g

CARROT CAKE BALLS

- ½ cup old rolled oats
- 1 cup dates, pitted
- ¼ tsp. turmeric
- ½ tsp. ground cinnamon
- 1 tsp. vanilla
- 2 medium carrots, grated
- ¼ cup chia seeds
- ¼ cup pecans, chopped
- ¼ tsp. salt

Directions:

1. Add dates, chia seeds, pecans, and oats to the food processor and process until well combined.
2. Add remaining ingredients and process until just combined.
3. Make small balls with the oat mixture, arrange them on the plate, and place the plate in the refrigerator for 20 minutes. Serve cold and enjoy.

Ingredient tip: Add ½ tsp. ground ginger.

Prep 10 m	**Portion** 6	**Cook** 35 m	**Per Serving** *Calories 246; Fat 13g; Sat Fat: 6.5g; Carb 20g; Protein: 12g*

EGGPLANT CAKE

- 2 eggplants
- 1 tbsp extra virgin olive oil
- 3 1/2 ounces of feta cheese
- 3 1/2 ounces provolone cheese, grated
- 1 cooked and mashed potato
- 2 eggs

Directions:

1. preheat the oven to 350°F.

2. Place eggplant on a baking sheet and roast until evenly charred.

3. Carve a slit in the bottom of each eggplant and place it in a colander. Allow them to drain.

4. Once cool enough to handle, remove the charred skin from the eggplants, discard the dark seeds, and coarsely chop.

5. Mix the chopped eggplant with olive oil, cheeses, mashed potatoes, and eggs until smooth.

6. Place in a baking dish and bake for 35 minutes, until the surface is lightly browned.

7. Remove from oven and let cool for a few minutes before serving.

Serving tip: Serve with tomato sauce.

Substitution tip: Use boiled and chopped leeks instead of eggplant.

Prep 10 m	**Portion** 6	**Cook** 40 m	**Per Serving** *Calories 439; Fat 6g; Sat Fat: 0.9g; Carb 89g; Protein: 10g*

BAKED ITALIAN FRIES

- 12 baby red potatoes, cut into wedges
- 1 tbsp Italian seasoning
- 3 tbsp extra virgin olive oil
- 1 tsp turmeric
- ½ tsp of sea salt
- ½ tsp dried rosemary
- 1 tbsp dried dill

Directions:

1. Preheat the oven to 375°F

2. Place potato wedges in a large bowl.

3. Add the Italian seasoning, olive oil, turmeric, sea salt, dried rosemary, and dried dill. Mix well to coat the wedges.

4. Line a baking sheet with baking paper.

5. Arrange the potato wedges in the baking dish in a single layer.

6. Bake for 40 minutes, stirring the wedges occasionally with a spatula.

Serving tip: Garnish with sprigs of rosemary.

Substitution tip: You can add a little paprika.

Prep 10 m	**Portion** 6	**Cook** 0 m	**Per Serving** *Calories 125; Fat 9g; Sat Fat: 2.6g; Carb1g; Protein:70g*

MEDITERRANEAN DEVILED EGGS

- 6 large free-range eggs, hard-boiled
- 1/8 tsp white pepper
- 1/8 tsp kosher salt
- 1/2 tsp freshly squeezed lemon juice
- 1/8 tsp smoked sweet paprika
- 1/2 tsp finely grated lemon zest
- 1 tsp dried oregano
- 2 tbsp crumbled feta cheese
- 3 tbsp reduced-fat mayonnaise
- 12 pitted black olives

Directions:

1. Carefully cut the hard-boiled eggs and use a tsp to remove the yolks. Arrange the whites on a serving plate. Transfer 4 yolks to a medium-sized bowl, discard the others or freeze them for another use.

2. Add the pepper, salt, lemon juice, paprika, zest, oregano, cheese, and mayonnaise to the bowl with the yolks. Use a fork to beat and mash the mixture until it forms a smooth paste.

3. Pour the yolk mixture into the egg whites and garnish with olives before serving.

Prep
5 m

Makes
6

Cook
15 m

Per Serving
Calories 261; Fat 14g; Sat Fat: 2g; Carb 33g; Protein: 5g

VEGETARIAN PANCAKES

- 1/2 cup almond milk
- 1/2 cup of chickpea flour
- 6 tbsp extra virgin olive oil (divided)
- ½ tsp Kosher salt
- 8 oz. champignon mushrooms, stemless
- 3 sprigs of fresh thyme
- Freshly ground black pepper
- 1 bunch of Swiss chard, no ribs, finely chopped

Directions:

1. In a medium-sized bowl, whisk together the milk, flour, 2 tbsp olive oil, and a small pinch of salt until the batter is almost smooth. Let the batter rest for 15 minutes while you prepare the rest of the dish.

2. Heat 1 tbsp of olive oil in a large skillet over medium heat. When the oil is hot, add the mushrooms, thyme, 1/8 tsp salt, and a pinch of black pepper. Sauté the mushrooms for about 5 minutes, or until they darken. Scrape the cooked mushrooms into a bowl and keep warm.

3. Heat 1 tbsp oil in the same skillet and add the chard with another 1/8 tsp salt and another pinch of black pepper. Sauté the chard for about 5 minutes, or until all the leaves are wilted. Pour the cooked chard into the same bowl with the mushrooms and keep warm.

4. Wipe the greens and excess oil from the skillet using crumpled wax paper. Return the skillet to medium heat and add 1 tbsp of oil. When the oil is hot, whisk the batter once more to incorporate as much air as possible. Add half the batter to the hot oil, gently swirling the pan to coat the bottom.

5. Fry the pancake for 2-3 minutes before flipping and frying the other side until lightly browned (about 2-3 minutes). Flip the pancake onto a plate and repeat with the remaining oil and batter.

6. Serve the pancakes hot and topped with cooked mushrooms and chard.

Prep
10 m

Portion
24 Makes

Cook
15 m

Per Serving
Calories 45; Fat 4g; Sat Fat: 1g; Carb 1g; Protein: 1g

ITALIAN BRUSCHETTA

- 6 kalamata olives, pitted and chopped
- 2 tbsp green onion, chopped
- ¼ cup grated Parmesan cheese, divided by two
- ¼ cup extra virgin olive oil for brushing or as needed
- ¼ cup cherry tomatoes, thinly sliced
- 1 tsp lemon juice
- 1 tbsp extra virgin olive oil
- 1 tbsp basil pesto
- 1 red bell pepper, cut in half and stripped of seeds
- 1 piece (12 inches) whole-wheat baguette, cut into half-inch-thick slices
- 1 package (4 ounces) feta cheese with basil and sun-dried tomatoes, crumbled
- 1 clove of garlic, chopped

Directions:

1. Set the grill to medium and place the oven rack 6 inches below the heat source.

2. Brush both sides of baguette slices with ¼ cup olive oil.

3. Place the bread slices on a baking sheet; toast them in the oven for about 1 minute on each side, being careful not to burn them.

4. Remove the toasted slices and transfer them to another baking sheet.

5. With cut sides down, place red peppers on a baking sheet; bake for about 8 to 10 minutes or until skin is charred and crumbled.

6. Transfer roasted peppers to a bowl; cover with plastic wrap.

7. Allow peppers to cool, then remove the charred skin. Discard skin and cut off roasted peppers.

8. Mix roasted red peppers, cherry tomatoes, feta, green onion, olives, pesto, 1 tbsp olive oil, garlic, and lemon juice in a bowl.

9. Top each loaf with a tbsp of roasted bell pepper mixture and sprinkle lightly with Parmesan cheese.

10. Bake for 2 minutes or until topping is lightly browned.

Serving tip: Add chopped green onions and fresh basil.

Substitution tip: Substitute whole wheat baguette for whole wheat sourdough starter.

Prep
10 m

Portion
15

Cook
1 h

Per Serving

Calories: 113; Total fat: 9g; Carb: 3g; Protein: 5g;
Sodium: 122g; Fiber: 2g

CHARD PIE WITH CHEESE AND ALMOND CRUST

- 3 tbsp. fresh water
- 1 tbsp. flaxseed meal (plus 2 tbsp.)
- Freshly ground black pepper
- 1/8 tsp. Kosher salt (plus 1/4 tsp.)
- 1/2 tsp. dried oregano
- 1 cup almond flour
- 1 tbsp. avocado oil
- 1 tbsp. extra virgin olive oil
- 2 tbsp. crushed garlic
- 1/2 medium shallot, finely chopped
- 10 ounces Swiss chard
- 1/2 tsp. dried oregano
- 5 ounces soft goat cheese, grated
- 2 large free-range eggs
- 1/4 cup almond slivers

Directions:

1. Set oven to preheat to 350degreesF, with rack in center of oven. Spray a large casserole dish with baking spray and set it aside.

2. Place the water in a medium-sized bowl, along with the flaxseed meal, and combine gently. Lightly whisk in a pinch of freshly ground black pepper, along with the salt, oregano, and almond flour. Add the oil and mix until the ingredients form a dough. Use your hands to bring the dough together and press it tightly into the prepared casserole dish. Press down the sides as well to form a rim. Bake the crust in the oven for about 18 minutes or golden brown.

3. Meanwhile, heat the olive oil in a large saucepan over medium-low heat.

When the oil is hot, sauté the garlic and shallots for about 5 minutes, or until the shallots are tender and translucent. Add the chard and sauté for about 2 minutes until the chard has reduced.

4. Transfer the pan to a wooden cutting board and stir in the remaining 1/4 tsp. salt, a large pinch of pepper, oregano, cheese, and egg.

5. Pour the filling into the pre-cooked crust and sprinkle with the almond slivers before returning the pie to the oven and baking for another 28 minutes, or until the filling is firm and the almonds are lightly toasted.

6. Slice and serve warm, or chill for a tasty snack.

Ingredient Tip: You can add a little nutmeg powder to add more taste.

Prep
10 m

Portion
2

Cook
20 m

Per Serving

Calories: 290 calories; Fat: 14 g; Sat. Fat: 2 g; Carb: 34 g; Protein: 12 g;
Fiber: 6 g

FETA SPINACH AND SWEET RED PEPPER MUFFINS

- 1/3 cup baby spinach leaves
- 1 tbsp. red peppers, jarred, patted dry
- 2/3 cups whole-wheat flour
- 1 tbsp. coconut sugar
- ¼ tsp. salt
- ½ tsp. paprika
- ½ tsp. baking powder
- 1 ½ tbsp. extra-virgin olive oil
- 1 medium egg, at room temperature
- 1 tbsp. almond milk, low-fat, unsweetened
- 1 tbsp. crumbled feta cheese, low-fat

Directions

1. Switch on the oven, set it to 190 degrees C or 375 degrees F, and preheat.

2. Meanwhile, take six silicone muffin cups, line them with muffin liners, and spray them with cooking spray to grease them.

3. Take a medium bowl, add flour, sugar, salt, paprika, and baking powder and stir until mixed.

4. Take a medium bowl, crack an egg in it, pour in the oil and milk, and whisk until mixed.

5. Then add the prepared egg mixture into the flour mixture, ½ cup at a time, stir until combined, and thick dough formed.

6. Add feta cheese, spinach, and red peppers, stir until incorporated, and divide the mixture evenly among the prepared muffin cups.

7. Place the muffin cups in the oven, and bake for 20 to 25 minutes, or until firm and the top turns golden brown.

8. When done, let the muffin cool at room temperature for 5 minutes and then serve.

Substitution tip: You can replace feta cheese with goat cheese.

Prep
10 m

Portion
4-6

Cook
10 m

Per Serving
Calories: 237; Total fat: 14g; Saturated fat: 2g; Carb: 18g; Protein: 11g; Sodium: 655mg; Fiber: 3g

PUMPKIN PANCAKES COVERED WITH YOGURT

- 6 small yellow pumpkins, grated
- 1 1/4 tsp. Himalayan salt (divided)
- 1/2 lemon, squeezed
- 2 tbsp. sweet smoked paprika
- 1 cup plain Greek yogurt
- 1/4 tsp. white pepper
- 1/2 cup whole-wheat flour
- 3 large free-range eggs, beaten
- 4 spring onions, thinly sliced
- 1/4 cup fresh parsley, finely chopped
- 4 ounces feta cheese, crumbled
- olive oil for frying

Directions:

1. Mix grated squash in a large bowl with 1 tsp. salt. Transfer it to a colander set over the sink and let it drain for at least 20 minutes. Use a wooden spoon or ladle's back to gently press excess water from the vegetables before transferring them back to a bowl.

2. In a small glass bowl, whisk the lemon juice, paprika, yogurt, and 1/4 tsp. salt. Set aside.

3. Add the pepper, flour, eggs, spring onions, parsley, and crumbled feta to the bowl with the squash, stirring gently to combine.

4. In a large skillet over medium-high heat, heat 1/2 inch of oil. Test the oil by inserting the tip of a toothpick - the oil is ready when the toothpick immediately begins to sizzle. Use a spoon to carefully drop the batter into the hot oil - about 4-5 pancakes at a time. Flatten the pancakes slightly with a spatula and fry for 2 minutes. Flip and fry the other side for another 2 minutes, or until both sides are lightly browned.

5. Transfer the cooked pancakes to a serving plate and keep warm.

6. Serve the pancakes warm, topped with the yogurt dressing.

Substitution tip: You can replace feta cheese with goat cheese.

Prep
20 m

Portion
2

Cook
5 m

Per Serving
Calories: 282; Fat: 10.4g; Sat fat: 3.6g; Carb: 39.2g; Fiber: 8.4g; Sugar: 6.8g; Protein: 10.4g

VEGETARIAN TORTILLA WRAPS

- ½ small zucchini, thinly sliced
- ½ tsp. olive oil
- ½ medium red bell pepper, seeded and thinly sliced
- 2 whole-wheat tortillas
- ½ cup fresh spinach
- 1 tsp. dried oregano
- 1 red onion, thinly sliced
- ¼ cup hummus
- 2 tbsp. feta cheese, crumbled
- 1 tbsp. black olives, pitted and sliced

Directions:

1. Heat the olive oil in a small skillet over medium-low heat. Add the bell pepper, zucchini, and onion.

2. Sauté for about 5 minutes.

3. Meanwhile, in another skillet, heat the tortillas one by one until hot.

4. Place hummus evenly in the center of each wrapper.

5. Place the spinach on each tortilla, then add the sautéed vegetables, feta cheese, oregano, and olives.

6. Carefully fold the edges of each tortilla over the filling and roll-up.

7. Cut each roll in half crosswise and serve.

Ingredient Tip: Serve with a healthy sauce of your choice.

Substitution tip: You can also use corn tortillas.

Prep
10 m

Portion
4

Cook
8 m

Per Serving
Calories 152; Fat 11g; Sodium 520mg; Carb 1g; Fiber 0g; Sugar 0.2g; Protein 12g

CRISPY CHEESE

- ¾ cup cheddar cheese, shredded
- ¾ cup Parmesan cheese, shredded
- 1 tsp. Italian seasoning

Directions:

1. Mix cheese and spread on a baking sheet.

2. Bake for eight minutes in a 400degreesF oven.

Serving tip: Serve with marinara sauce.

Ingredient Tip: Add some dried herbs and ground spices to add more taste.

| **Prep** | **Portion** | **Cook** | **Per Serving (2 tartlets)** |
| 5 m | 15 Makes | 12 m | Calories 141; Fat 4g; Sat Fat:2g; Carb21g; Protein:3g |

SPICY CRAB CHUNKS

- 30 miniature frozen phyllo dough shells
- 1/2 tsp of seafood seasoning
- 1/2 cup reduced-fat vegetable cream cheese spread
- 1/2 tsp freshly ground black pepper
- 1/3 tsp cayenne pepper
- 1/3 cup crab meat, drained
- 5 tbsp hot sauce

Directions:

1. Bake the tartlets according to package instructions and allow them to cool completely on a wire rack.

2. Whisk together the seafood seasoning, cream cheese, black pepper, and cayenne pepper in a medium-sized bowl. Gently stir in the crabmeat until all ingredients are well combined.

3. Spread the mixture into the cooled phyllo shells and top with a few sprinkles of hot sauce before serving.

| **Prep** | **Portion** | **Cook** | **Per Serving** |
| 5 m | 16 Makes | 3 m | Calories 89; Fat 5g; Sat Fat:0.1g; Carb 1g; Protein:11g |

ROAST BEEF AND ASPARAGUS INVOLTINI

- 16 fresh asparagus, cut
- 1/8 tsp ground cumin
- 1 tsp lemon juice
- 1 tsp French mustard
- 1 tsp crushed garlic
- 1/3 cup mayonnaise
- 8 thin slices of roast beef cut in half lengthwise
- 3 medium peppers of different colors, thinly sliced
- 16 whole herbs
- Freshly ground black pepper

Directions:

1. Bring a small pot of water to a boil. When the water boils, add the asparagus and boil for no more than 3 minutes. Drain the asparagus immediately after cooking and place it in a bowl with ice water. Drain again and dry completely.

2. Whisk together the cumin, lemon juice, mustard, garlic, and mayonnaise in a small glass bowl.

3. Arrange the roast beef slices on a clean work surface. Top each slice of roast beef with 1 tsp of the mayonnaise mixture, using the back of a tsp to distribute it. Place 1 asparagus on each slice of beef and top with bell pepper slices of each color. Sprinkle with black pepper before rolling the bundles and securing them with chive strands.

4. Serve immediately.

| **Prep** | **Portion** | **Cook** | **Per Serving** |
| 5 m | 4 | 0 m | Calories 88; Fat 3g; Sat Fat: 2g; Carb 11g; Protein: 4g |

CHICKPEAS HUMMUS

- 1 cup cooked chickpeas
- ½ tsp. minced garlic
- 2 tbsp. tahini paste
- 2 tsp. lemon juice
- 2 cubes of ice
- ½ tsp. sea salt
- ½ tsp. lemon pepper seasoning
- 2 tsp. extra-virgin olive oil

Directions

1. Plug in a food processor, add chickpeas and garlic, and pulse for 30 seconds or more until smooth and powder-like consistency.

2. Then add tahini, salt, ice cube, and lemon juice, and pulse until the mixture is well combined and smooth.

3. When done, spoon the hummus into a bowl, drizzle oil on it, sprinkle with the lemon pepper seasoning, and serve with favorite crackers and vegetable slices.

Prep	Portion	Cook	Per Serving
10 m	4	5 m	

Per Serving

Calories: 268; Fat: 16.9g; Sat fat: 8.3g; Carb: 25g; Fiber: 6.2g; Sugar: 8.7g; Protein: 7.4g

GRILLED VEGETARIAN PANINI

- ¼ cup mayonnaise
- Olive oil cooking spray
- ½ tsp. fresh lemon juice
- 2 small zucchini, thinly sliced lengthwise
- 2 portobello mushrooms, cut into ¼-inch-thick slices
- Salt, to taste
- ½ cup feta cheese, crumbled
- 2 cups fresh arugula
- 2 cloves garlic, minced
- 1 eggplant, cut into quarter-inch-thick slices
- 2 tbsp. olive oil
- ¾ of a ciabatta loaf, split horizontally
- 2 medium tomatoes, sliced

Directions:

1. Set the broiler on high and grease a baking sheet with cooking spray.
2. In a bowl, add the mayonnaise, garlic, and lemon juice and mix well. Set aside.
3. Evenly coat the zucchini, eggplant, and mushrooms with the oil and sprinkle with salt.
4. Arrange the vegetable slices on the baking sheet and bake for about 1 1/2 minutes per side.
5. Move the vegetable slices to a plate.
6. Place loaves on a grill, cut side down, and bake for about 2 minutes.
7. Remove from grill and cut each half loaf into four equal-sized pieces.
8. Spread the mayonnaise mixture evenly over each piece of bread and top with the vegetable slices, followed by the tomatoes, arugula, and feta cheese.
9. Top with the top pieces and serve. Serve these sandwiches with your favorite sauce.

Substitution tip: Any type of mushrooms can be used.

Prep	Makes	Cook
5 m	16	0 m

Per Serving

Calories: 63; Total fat: 3g; Saturated fat: 0g; Carb: 7g; Protein: 1g; Sodium: 183mg;

MEDITERRANEAN TAPENADE

- 1/4 tsp. dried thyme
- 3 tbsp. crushed garlic
- 1 tbsp. capers, drained
- 1 tbsp. fresh parsley, chopped
- 2 tbsp. extra virgin olive oil
- 2 tbsp. freshly squeezed lime juice
- 1/4 cup chopped poblano peppers
- 1/2 cup black olives, pitted
- 1/2 cup red peppers, chopped
- 16 thin slices of French baguette, lightly toasted

Directions:

1. Place the thyme, garlic, capers, parsley, olive oil, lime juice, poblano peppers, and olives in a food processor and give it a full pulse until you have a smooth paste.
2. Spread about 1 tbsp. of tapenade on each lightly toasted baguette slice and serve.

Substitution Tip: Black olives can be replaced with green olives.

Notes.

....

....

....

....

|
Prep
5 m |
Portion
2 |
Cook
15 m |
Per Serving
Calories: 238 calories; Fat: 7.8 g; Sat. Fat: 1 g; Carb: 32 g; Protein: 10.6 g; Fiber: 6.4 g |

ROASTED CHICKPEAS

- 2 cups of cooked chickpeas
- 1/3 tsp. salt
- ¼ tsp. dried oregano
- ¼ tsp. garlic powder
- ¼ tsp. ground black pepper
- 1 tbsp. olive oil
- 1 tsp. red wine vinegar
- 1 tsp. lemon juice

Directions

1. Turn on the oven, set it to 218 degrees C or 425 degrees F, and let it preheat.
2. Take a baking sheet, line it with baking paper, and arrange the chickpeas in a single layer.
3. Place the baking sheet in the oven and roast the chickpeas for 10 minutes until they are tender, crispy, and golden brown, turning them halfway through cooking.
4. Take a large bowl, place salt, black pepper, oregano, garlic powder, black pepper, oil, red wine vinegar, and lemon juice, and mix until combined.
5. Add the roasted chickpeas, stir until well combined, and then arrange the chickpea mixture on the baking sheet.
6. Return to the oven and continue roasting for 5 minutes or until golden brown.
7. When done, pour the mixture into a serving bowl and serve.

|
Prep
10 m |
Portion
4 |
Cook
0 m |
Per Serving
Calories: 223; Total fat: 19.7g; Saturated fat: 7g; Carb: 5.7g; Protein: 6.4g; Fiber: 0.7g |

ZESTY CUCUMBER AND YOGURT DIP

- 1 medium English cucumber
- 1/2 small fennel bulb
- Freshly ground black pepper
- Sea salt
- 2 tbsp. fresh dill, chopped
- 1 tsp. crushed garlic
- 1 tbsp. lemon zest, finely grated
- 2 tbsp. freshly squeezed lemon juice
- 5 tbsp. avocado oil (divided)
- 2 cups plain Greek yogurt

Directions:

1. Grate the cucumber into a large bowl and use the back of a wooden spoon to press out and drain excess liquid.
2. Place the fennel bulb in a food processor and puree on high until finely chopped. Scrape the chopped fennel bulb into the bowl with the cucumber.
3. Season the chopped cucumber and fennel with a large pinch of salt and pepper. Stir in the dill, garlic, zest, lemon juice, 3 tbsp. oil, and yogurt until all ingredients are well combined. Drizzle with the remaining oil and serve.

Ingredient Tip: Leftover sauce can be stored in the refrigerator, in an airtight container, for no more than 5 days.

Soup & Stew

RICE SOUP WITH CHICKEN AND CHARD

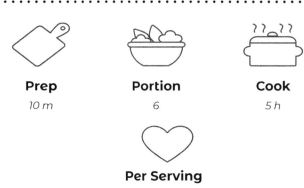

Prep
10 m

Portion
6

Cook
5 h

Per Serving

Calories 240; Fat 3g; Sat Fat: 0.8g; Carb 27g; Protein: 26g

Ingredients:
- 1/4 tsp kosher salt
- 1/2 tsp freshly ground black pepper
- 1/2 tsp dried thyme
- 1 tsp crushed garlic
- 2/3 cup uncooked wild rice
- 10 oz. of reduced-fat, low-sodium, undiluted canned condensed chicken cream
- 14.5 oz. low-sodium canned chicken broth
- 3 cups hot water
- 2 cups beets, stemless, cut into chunks
- 3 cups cooked and diced chicken breast

Directions:
1. In a large pot, stir the salt, pepper, thyme, garlic, rice, chicken broth, and water. Cook the soup on low heat for 5-7 hours, or until the rice has softened.
2. Add the chard and chicken to the pot, stirring to combine. Cook for another 15 minutes, or until the chard is wilted. At this point, the chicken should be well cooked.
3. Pour the soup into bowls and serve hot.

Prep	Portion	Cook	Per Serving
20 m	6	1h 15 m	Calories 162; Fat 6g; Sat Fat: 0.8g; Carb 26g; Protein: 6g

SPICY LENTIL SOUP

- 2 carrots, peeled and chopped
- 2 tbsp extra virgin olive oil
- 2 stalks of celery, chopped
- 3 cloves of garlic, chopped
- 1 can of low-sodium diced tomatoes (14½ ounces)
- ¼ tsp dried oregano, chopped
- 1 tsp ground cumin
- ½ tsp paprika
- 3 cups fresh spinach, chopped
- 2 tbsp fresh lemon juice
- Salt and black pepper to taste
- 2 sweet onions, chopped
- 1½ cups brown lentils, picked and rinsed
- ¼ tsp dried basil, chopped
- ¼ tsp dried thyme, chopped
- ½ tsp ground cilantro
- 6 cups low-sodium vegetable broth

Directions:

1. In a large soup pot set over medium heat, add the carrots, celery, and onion.
2. Cook for about 5 minutes, then add the garlic.
3. Sauté for about 1 minute and add the brown lentils, stirring for about 3 minutes.
4. Add the tomatoes, herbs, spices and broth and let the mixture boil.
5. Reduce the heat to low, partially cover and simmer for about 1 hour.
6. Add the spinach, salt and black pepper and cook for about 4 minutes.
7. Squeeze in the lemon juice and serve hot.

Serving tip: You can serve the soup together with your favorite rice.
Substitution tip: yellow lentils can also be used.

Prep	Portion	Cook	Per Serving
5 m	2	20 m	Calories: 245 calories; Fat: 4.9 g; Sat. Fat: 0.5 g; Carb: 38.1 g; Protein: 12 g; Fiber: 11.2 g

WHITE BEAN SOUP

- ¾ cup spinach, sliced
- ½ of a medium white onion, peeled, chopped
- ½ of a medium stalk celery, chopped
- ½ of a medium carrot, chopped
- ½ tsp. minced garlic
- 12-ounce cooked white kidney beans
- ¼ tsp. ground black pepper
- ¼ tsp. dried thyme
- 1 tsp. extra-virgin olive oil
- 7 ounces chicken broth
- 1 tsp. lemon juice
- 1 cup water

Directions

1. Take a medium saucepan, place it over medium heat, add oil, add celery, carrot, and onion, and cook for 5 minutes or until softened.
2. Add garlic, cook for a minute until golden, add beans, black pepper, thyme, pour in the broth and water, stir until mixed, and then bring it to a boil.
3. Cook the soup for 10 minutes, remove half of the beans and vegetables from the prepared soup and set it aside until required.
4. Remove pan from heat and then pulse it with an electric hand mixer until smooth.
5. Return the saucepan over medium heat, bring the soup to a boil, add spinach, and lemon juice, cook for 3 to 4 minutes until spinach leaves have wilted.
6. When done, divide the soup evenly between two bowls, and serve.

Prep	Portion	Cook	Per Serving
5 m	2	35 m	Calories 202; Fat 14g; Sat Fat: 1.3g; Carb 18g; Protein: 6g

LENTIL SOUP

- 4 tbsp. minced onion
- ½ of a large carrot, chopped
- 1 tsp. minced garlic
- 4-ounce brown lentils
- 1 bay leaf
- ¼ tsp. sea salt
- ¼ tsp. ground black pepper
- ¼ tsp. dried rosemary
- ¼ tsp. dried oregano
- 2 tbsp. extra virgin olive oil, divided
- 1 tsp. tomato paste
- 2 tbsp. water and more as needed

Directions

1. Take a medium pot, place it over medium heat, add lentils, pour in enough water to cover lentils by 1-inch over the lentils, and cook for 10 minutes.
2. When lentils have been cooked, drain them, transfer them into a medium bowl, and set them aside until required.
3. Take a medium saucepan, place it over medium heat, add oil, and when hot, add garlic, onion, and carrot, and cook for 3 to 4 minutes until softened.
4. Then add lentils, oregano, rosemary, and bay leaf, pour in the water, and then bring the soup to a boil.
5. Then switch heat to medium-low level, cover the pot with its lid, and continue simmering the soup for 5 minutes.
6. Then add tomato paste, salt, and black pepper, stir until mixed, cover the pot with its lid, and let it cook for 15 minutes, or until lentils have turned soft.
7. When done, divide the soup evenly between two bowls, drizzle oil on top, and serve.

Prep
10 m

Portion
4-6

Cook
15 m

Per Serving
Calories: 287; Total fat: 7g; Carb: 40g; Protein: 14g; Sodium: 576 mg; Fiber: 15g

CARROT AND LENTIL SOUP

- *2 tbsp. extra virgin avocado oil (extra for garnish)*
- *1 tsp. crushed garlic*
- *1 cup shallots, chopped*
- *1 medium carrot, thinly sliced*
- *1/4 tsp. dried oregano*
- *1/2 tsp. smoked sweet paprika*
- *1/2 tsp. ground cumin*
- *4 cups vegetable broth*
- *1 cup lentils, thoroughly rinsed and drained*
- *4 lemon slices*
- *Himalayan salt*
- *White pepper*

Directions:

1.   *Heat the oil in a large pot over medium heat. When the oil is nice and hot, add garlic, scallions, and carrots. Lower the heat and sauté for about 5 minutes or until the carrots soften. Stir in the oregano, paprika, and cumin for 30 seconds.*

2.   *Add the broth and lentils. Place a lid on the pot, leaving a small space for steam to escape. Let the soup simmer for 15 minutes, occasionally stirring until the lentils soften. When the lentils are cooked, turn off the stove and stir in the lemon slices. Taste the soup and add more salt and a pinch of pepper, if necessary.*

3.   *Pour the soup into bowls and garnish with a few drops of oil, if desired. Serve warm.*

Prep
20 m

Portion
8

Cook
25 m

Per Serving
Calories: 105; Fat: 1.3g; Sat fat: 0.3g; Carb: 19.2g; Fiber: 4.6g; Sugar: 9.2g; Protein: 5.7g

VEGETARIAN SOUP

- *4 small zucchini, chopped*
- *2 (14-ounce) cans diced tomatoes with juice (low sodium)*
- *8 carrots, peeled and chopped*
- *4 small onions, chopped*
- *1 leek, chopped*
- *1 tsp. ground cumin*
- *¼ tsp. paprika*
- *1 slice of whole-wheat bread, toasted and cut into small croutons*
- *2 cloves of garlic, minced*
- *¼ tsp. ground cayenne pepper*
- *Sea Salt and black pepper, to taste*
- *4¼ cups vegetable broth*

Directions:

1.   *Add all ingredients except croutons in a large soup pot set over high heat. Allow the mixture to boil.*

2.   *Reduce heat to low, partially cover, and simmer for about 20 minutes.*

3.   *Remove from heat and set aside to cool slightly.*

4.   *In batches, pour the soup into a blender and blend until smooth.*

5.   *Transfer the puree to the same skillet over medium heat and let it simmer for about 4 minutes.*

6.   *Remove from heat and serve topped with croutons.*

Ingredient Tip: *Serve with a garnish of fresh parsley.*
Substitution Tip: You can use any vegetable of your choice.

Notes.

....

....

....

....

....

Prep
10 m

Portion
4

Cook
30 m

Per Serving
Calories 473; Fat 9g; Sat Fat: 1.5g; Carb 83g; Protein: 2g

MOROCCAN LENTIL STEW

- *2 tbsp avocado oil*
- *1 tbsp curry powder*
- *1 tbsp ground turmeric*
- *1 tbsp ground cumin*
- *¼ tbsp kosher salt*
- *1 large shallot, diced*
- *4 tbsp crushed garlic*
- *2 tbsp fresh ginger, chopped*
- *1 red bell pepper, seeded and diced*
- *1 kg diced squash*
- *6 cups vegetable broth*
- *1 1/2 cups red lentils, rinsed and drained*
- *1/4 cup fresh cilantro leaves, chopped, for garnish*

Directions:

1. In a large pot over medium heat, heat oil before adding curry powder, turmeric, and cumin. Stir for 1 minute so that the flavors blend. Add the salt, scallions, and sauté for 5 minutes until the scallions become translucent. Add the garlic and ginger for another 2 minutes. Add the peppers and pumpkin cubes to the pot, stirring to combine. Finally, add the broth and lentils and stir until the stew starts to simmer.

2. Lower the heat to maintain a gentle simmer and cook with the lid on for 20 minutes, occasionally stirring, until the lentils have softened.

3. Pour the soup into bowls and serve hot, garnished with chopped cilantro leaves.

Prep
10 m

Portion
4

Cook
20 m

Per Serving
Calories 365; Fat 14g; Sat Fat: 0.8g; Carb 37g; Protein: 32g

BEEF STEW

- *28 oz. Canned low-sodium beef broth.*
- *3/4 lb. lean ground beef*
- *1/3 tsp. red pepper flakes*
- *1/2 tsp. dried thyme*
- *1 tsp. crushed garlic*
- *1 tbsp. of currents*
- *1/2 cup V8 juice*
- *1 small shallot, finely chopped*
- *2 medium sweet potatoes, peeled and diced (1/2-inch cubes)*

Directions:

1. Bring beef broth to a boil in a large pot over medium-high heat. Stir in the ground beef. Place a lid on the pot, and cook for 3 minutes, stirring at regular intervals to avoid burning.

2. Remove the lid and stir in the red pepper flakes, thyme, garlic, currents, V8 juice, shallots, and sweet potatoes. Stir the stew for a few minutes until the sauce begins to boil again. Once the sauce boils, lower the heat to maintain a gentle simmer. Let the stew simmer for 15 minutes, occasionally stirring, until the beef is cooked through and the sweet potatoes are fork-tender.

3. Pour soup into bowls and serve hot.

Notes.

....

....

....

....

....

Prep	Portion	Cook	Per Serving
10 m	4	45 m	*Calories: 270; Total fat: 8g; Carb: 20g; Protein: 25g; Sodium: 713 mg; Fiber: 3g*

BEEF STEW BRAISED IN RED WINE

- 1 tbsp. extra virgin avocado oil.
- 1 pound beef stew, cut into chunks
- 8 ounces button mushrooms, diced
- 3 tbsp. of tomato paste
- 1/2 cup dry red wine
- 3 1/2 cups beef broth (divided)
- 1 tsp. Italian seasoning
- 2 tsp. crushed garlic
- 1 medium carrot, cut into half-moons
- 1/2 medium shallot, diced
- 2 medium russet potatoes, diced
- 1/4 tsp. Kosher salt
- White pepper
- 1 tsp. arrowroot
- Fresh chives, chopped

Directions:

1. In a large pot over medium-high heat, heat the oil. When the oil is nice and hot, scrape the beef cubes into it, and fry for about 5 minutes, or until the cubes are nicely browned on all sides. Add the mushrooms and fry for another 5 minutes until the mushrooms are darker. Stir in the tomato paste for 1 minute. Add the wine to the pot and bring to a gentle boil, scraping up any bits of food that may have remained in the bottom of the pot. When the wine has been reduced by half, add 3 1/4 cups of beef broth to the pot, stirring to combine.

2. Stir in the Italian seasoning, garlic, carrots, scallions, potatoes, salt, and a generous pinch of pepper. Let the stew simmer for about 25 minutes, or until the vegetables are fork-tender, stirring occasionally.

3. Whisk the arrowroot with the remaining beef broth in a medium-sized bowl until dissolved. Whisk the mixture into the stew and simmer for another 5 minutes.

4. Pour the stew into bowls and serve warm, garnished with fresh chives.

Prep	Portion	Cook	Per Serving
15 m	6	25 m	*Calories: 170; Fat: 13.1g; Sat fat: 3.2g; Carb: 9.6g; Fiber: 2.5g; Sugar: 4.5g; Protein: 6g*

ZUCCHINI AND BASIL SOUP

- 2½ pounds zucchini, chopped
- 2 tbsp. extra-virgin olive oil
- 1 medium onion, chopped
- 4 cloves garlic, minced
- ⅓ cup fresh basil leaves, chopped
- ⅓ cup heavy cream
- 4 cups chicken broth
- Salt and black pepper, to taste
- 2 tbsp. extra virgin olive oil

Directions:

1. In a large skillet over medium-low heat, add olive oil, zucchini, and onion.

2. Cook for about 6 minutes, stirring often.

3. Add the garlic and sauté for about 1 minute.

4. Add the chicken broth and let simmer over medium-high heat.

5. Reduce heat to medium-low and simmer for about 15 minutes.

6. Sprinkle with basil, salt, and black pepper and remove from heat.

7. Blend the soup with an immersion blender until it forms a smooth puree.

8. Ladle the soup into serving bowls and drizzle with extra virgin olive oil.

9. Add the heavy cream and serve immediately.

Ingredient Tip: Serve with slices of toasted whole-wheat bread.

Substitution tip: Vegetable broth can be used instead of chicken broth.

Prep	Portion	Cook	Per Serving
10 m	8	6 h	*Calories: 111; Total fat: 0g; Saturated fat: 0g; Carb: 21g; Protein: 8g; Sodium: 537 mg; Fiber: 6g*

ITALIAN STYLE BEAN AND CABBAGE SOUP

4 cups chicken broth
6 ounces canned tomato paste
1/2 tsp. Sea salt
1 whole bay leaf
2 sprigs of fresh thyme
2 tsp. crushed garlic
15.5 ounces white beans, drained and rinsed

1 small shallot, chopped
2 large carrots, chopped
4 celery stalks, chopped
1 1/2 pounds cabbage, shredded
Parmesan cheese, grated, for garnish

Directions:

1. In a large saucepan over low heat, whisk together the chicken broth and tomato paste until adequately combined. Stir in the salt, bay leaf, thyme sprigs, garlic, beans, scallions, carrots, celery, and cabbage, until all ingredients are well combined. Place the lid on the pot over low heat and simmer for 6-8 hours, until the vegetables are fork-tender.

2. Discard the bay leaf and thyme sprigs. Pour the soup into bowls and serve hot, garnished with Parmesan cheese.

Prep	Portion	Cook	Per Serving
5 m	4	15 m	Calories 387; Fat7g; Sat Fat: 3.6g; Carb 38g; Protein: 50g

CHICKPEA AND PASTA SOUP

- 15 oz. canned chickpeas, drained and rinsed
- 4 cups chicken broth
- pinch of saffron
- 1 tsp kosher salt
- 1/3 cup avocado oil
- 6 oz. farfalle pasta, cooked according to package instructions and thoroughly drained

Directions:

1. Bring the chickpeas and broth to a boil in a large pot over medium-high heat. Lower the heat and simmer for 10 minutes until the chickpeas have softened, stirring regularly to prevent burning. Add the saffron and salt, stirring to incorporate.

2. While the soup simmers, add the avocado oil to a large skillet and heat over medium-high heat. Once the cooked pasta has been in the colander and is very dry, add 1/3 of the pasta to the hot oil and fry for about 3 minutes, until the edges are nice and crispy. Transfer the crispy dough to a plate lined with paper towels with a slotted spoon. Save the oil for serving.

3. Stir the remaining cooked pasta into the soup pot.

4. Pour the soup into bowls and garnish with the crispy noodles and a few drops of the frying oil. Serve hot, and enjoy!

Prep	Portion	Cook	Per Serving
10 m	6	30 m	Calories 238; Fat 19g; Sat Fat: 5g; Carb 17g; Protein: 43g

MINESTRONE SOUP

- 2 tbsp. extra virgin olive oil
- ⅓ cup Parmesan cheese, shredded
- 4 cloves garlic, chopped
- 1 onion, chopped
- Salt and black pepper, to taste
- 1 tsp. dried basil
- 14 ounces of crushed tomatoes
- 28 ounces diced tomatoes
- 6 cups chicken broth
- 2 celery stalks, chopped
- ⅓ pound green beans, chopped
- 1 carrot, diced
- 1 tsp. dried oregano
- 1 cup elbow pasta
- 15 ounces kidney beans
- 2 tbsp. fresh basil, chopped

Directions:

1. Sauté onions in heated olive oil over medium heat for five minutes.

2. Add garlic and cook for half a minute.

3. Add the carrot and celery and cook for another five minutes, stirring occasionally.

4. Add the oregano, green beans, salt, basil, and black pepper and cook for another three minutes, stirring constantly.

5. Pour in the broth followed by the tomatoes and let it simmer.

6. Lower the heat to low and let simmer for ten minutes.

7. Add the pasta and beans and cook for another ten minutes.

8. Add a little salt and serve.

Tip: Garnish with parmesan cheese and basil.

Ingredient Tip: Feel free to add any vegetables that are in season.

Prep	Portion	Cook	Per Serving
10 m	8	7 h (Slow Heat)	Calories 252; Fat12g; Sat Fat: 3.4g; Carb 4g; Protein: 29g

MUSHROOM AND CHICKEN SOUP

- 3 cups chicken breasts, diced
- 1 cup chicken broth
- 2 cups hot water
- 1 red onion, diced
- ¾ cup mushrooms, washed, dried, and sliced
- 4 cloves garlic, minced
- 1 tsp. dried oregano
- 1 can of diced Italian tomatoes
- 2 red peppers, sliced
- 1 tsp. ground cumin
- Salt and pepper to taste
- 2 tbsp. fresh parsley, chopped

Directions:

1. Preheat the slow stove to low.

2. Add all ingredients, then cover and cook low for 6 hours.

3. Break up the chicken with a fork, cover the slow stove again and cook for another hour until done.

4. Serve hot with a garnish of fresh parsley.

Ingredient Tip: Serve with sour cream.

Substitution Tip: Substitute red peppers for the yellow peppers.

Prep
10 m

Portion
4

Cook
1 h

Per Serving
Calories 244; Fat 17g; Sat Fat: 2g; Carb 13g; Protein: 57g

BOUILLABAISSE SOUP

1 lb. medium-large shrimp in the shell, thawed

1 tbsp garlic-flavored avocado oil (to add for drizzle)

1 tbsp crushed garlic

1/2 tsp cayenne pepper

1/2 cup dry white wine

1/4 cup chopped parsley (plus 2 whole stems)

1 whole bay leaf

1/4 tsp dried thyme

8 oz. of bottled clam juice

1/4 tsp flaked sea salt

14.5 oz. diced canned tomatoes

2 cups chicken broth

1/2 lb. tilapia, cut into 2-inch pieces

1/2 lemon, squeezed

Directions:

1. Remove shrimp from shell and place in a bowl, reserving shells and tails. Heat the oil in a large pot over medium heat and add the shells, tails, garlic, and cayenne pepper. Sauté for about 5 minutes until the flavors blend.

2. Add the white wine and simmer for 2 minutes, until half the wine has evaporated. Add 2 parsley stalks, bay leaf, thyme, and clam juice, stirring until the soup becomes a gentle simmer. Simmer for 15 to 30 minutes, lowering the heat until the soup thickens. Using a slotted spoon, remove all solid ingredients, including the shells, tails, parsley, and bay leaf.

3. Stir in the salt, tomatoes, and chicken broth, bringing the soup back to a gentle simmer. Stir in the shrimp and tilapia, ensuring the soup covers all the seafood. Set a timer for 3 minutes and simmer the soup with a lid on the pot. Keep an eye on the temperature to keep it simmering. The fish is cooked when it is completely solid. Transfer the pot to a wooden cutting board and stir the lemon juice.

4. Pour the soup into bowls and serve hot, garnished with chopped parsley and a few oil drizzles.

Prep
5 m

Portion
2

Cook
15 m

Per Serving
Calories: 307 calories; Fat: 4.8 g; Sat. Fat: 1.6 g; Carb: 53.6 g; Protein: 13.6 g; Fiber: 9.6 g

CHICKPEA SOUP PASTA

- 4 ounces cherry tomatoes, canned, drained
- ½ tsp. crushed dried rosemary
- 1 tsp. chopped garlic
- 12 ounces cooked chickpeas, divided
- 3 ounces whole-wheat pasta
- ¼ tsp. ground black pepper
- 1 tsp. olive oil
- 3 tbsp. grated Parmesan cheese, low-fat
- 15 ounces beef broth, sodium-reduced
- 1 cup water

Directions

1. Take a medium pot, place it over low heat, add oil and when hot, add garlic and cook for a minute until fragrant and golden.

2. Then add tomatoes, and rosemary, simmer for 3 minutes and then take a potato masher to crush the tomatoes.

3. Pour in the beef broth and water, switch the heat medium-high and bring the soup to a simmer.

4. Take a medium bowl, place half of the chickpeas, and with a potato masher, crush the chickpeas.

5. Add the crushed chickpeas into the soup and pasta and black pepper and stir until combined.

6. Let the soup simmer for 7 minutes or until the pasta has cooked, then add the remaining chickpeas into the soup, and stir until well mixed.

7. When done, spoon the prepared soup into a serving bowl, and serve.

Ingredient Tip: Add sage leaves to add more flavor.

Prep
10 m

Portion
6

Cook
30 m

Per Serving
Calories 260; Fat 8g; Sodium 961mg; Carb 37g; Fiber 10g; Sugar 10.2g; Protein 15g

ITALIAN MINESTRONE SOUP

- 2 tbsp. olive oil
- ⅓ cup Parmesan cheese, shredded
- 4 cloves garlic, chopped
- 1 onion, chopped
- 2 celery stalks, chopped
- ⅓ pound green beans, chopped
- 1 carrot, diced
- 1 tsp. dried oregano
- Salt and black pepper, to taste
- 1 tsp. dried basil
- 14 ounces of crushed tomatoes
- 28 ounces diced tomatoes
- 6 cups chicken broth
- 1 cup elbow pasta
- 15 ounces kidney beans
- 2 tbsp. fresh basil, chopped

Directions:

1. Sauté onions in heated olive oil over medium heat for five minutes.
2. Add garlic and cook for half a minute.
3. Add the carrot and celery and cook for another five minutes, stirring occasionally.
4. Add the oregano, green beans, salt, basil, and black pepper and cook for another three minutes, stirring constantly.
5. Pour in the broth followed by the tomatoes and let it simmer.
6. Lower the heat to low and let simmer for ten minutes.
7. Add the pasta and beans and cook for another ten minutes.
8. Add a little salt and serve.

Tip: Garnish with Parmesan cheese and basil.

Ingredient Tip: Feel free to add any vegetables that are in season.

Prep
10 m

Portion
4

Cook
20 m

Per Serving
Calories: 265; Total fat: 7g; Saturated fat: 3g; Carb: 29g; Protein: 20g; Sodium: 532 mg; Fiber: 4g

BEEF STEW

- 28 oz. Canned low-sodium beef broth.
- 3/4 lb. lean ground beef
- 1/3 tsp. red pepper flakes
- 1/2 tsp. dried thyme
- 1 tsp. crushed garlic
- 1 tbsp. of currents
- 1/2 cup V8 juice
- 1 small shallot, finely chopped
- 2 medium sweet potatoes, peeled and diced (1/2-inch cubes)

Directions:

1. Bring beef broth to a boil in a large pot over medium-high heat. Stir in the ground beef. Place a lid on the pot, and cook for 3 minutes, stirring at regular intervals to avoid burning.
2. Remove the lid and stir in the red pepper flakes, thyme, garlic, currents, V8 juice, shallots, and sweet potatoes. Stir the stew for a few minutes until the sauce begins to boil again. Once the sauce boils, lower the heat to maintain a gentle simmer. Let the stew simmer for 15 minutes, occasionally stirring, until the beef is cooked through and the sweet potatoes are fork-tender.
3. Pour soup into bowls and serve hot.

Prep
10 m

Portion
4

Cook
30 m

Per Serving
Calories 309; Fat 13g; Sodium 1984mg; Carb 32g; Fiber 5g; Sugar 17g; Protein 17g

BEET SOUP WITH CHEESE

- 1 tbsp. extra-virgin olive oil
- 6 large beets, peeled and cut into pieces
- 1 fennel bulb, coarsely chopped
- 1 sweet onion, chopped
- 1 tsp. chopped garlic
- 6 cups low-sodium chicken broth
- Sea salt and black pepper, to taste
- ½ cup goat cheese, crumbled
- 1 tbsp. fresh parsley, chopped

Directions:

1. In a saucepan, heat the olive oil over medium-high heat.
2. Sauté the beets, fennel, onion, and garlic until softened, occasionally stirring, about 10 minutes.
3. Add the chicken broth and bring the soup to a boil.
4. Reduce the heat to low and simmer until the vegetables are very tender, about 20 minutes.
5. Transfer the soup to a food processor or puree it until smooth using an immersion blender.
6. Return the soup to the casserole dish and season with salt and pepper.
7. Serve.

Ingredient Tip: Add the goat cheese and parsley.

Substitution Tip: Replace the chicken broth with vegetable broth.

Prep	Portion	Cook	Per Serving
5 m	5	20 m	*Calories 77; Fat 3g; Sat Fat: 0.4g; Carb 11g; Protein: 2g*

BEAN SOUP AND SPINACH

- 2 tbsp extra virgin olive oil
- 1 tbsp crushed garlic
- 1/2 medium shallot, diced
- 1 celery stalk, diced
- 1 medium carrot, diced
- 1/2 tbsp kosher salt
- White pepper
- 4 cups chopped spinach
- 1 tsp Italian seasoning
- 14.5 oz. diced canned tomatoes
- 3 cups vegetable broth
- 15 oz. canned northern beans, drained and rinsed
- 1 tbsp red wine vinegar

Directions:

1. Heat 2 tbsp of olive oil in a large pot over medium heat. When the oil is hot, add the garlic, scallions, celery, carrots, 1/4 tsp salt and a generous pinch of white pepper. Sauté the vegetables for 5 minutes before adding the spinach. Sauté for another 5 minutes, or until all the vegetables have softened.

2. Stir in the Italian seasoning, remaining salt, and another pinch of pepper. Add the canned tomatoes with their juice, vegetable broth, and northern beans. Let the soup simmer for 10 minutes, stirring at regular intervals and keeping an eye on the temperature. Add the red wine vinegar and stir.

Pour the soup into bowls and serve hot.

Prep	Portion	Cook	Per Serving
10 m	2	20 m	*Calories 434; Fat14g; Sat Fat: 0.4g; Carb 40g; Protein: 37g*

SALMON AND VEGETABLE SOUP

- 1 cup low-sodium chicken broth
- 1 1/2 cups hot water
- 1 large carrot, cut into thin slices (sliced 1/2 inch thick)
- 1 large Russian potato, cut into 1 1/2 inch thick pieces
- 1 cup champignon mushrooms, cut into thin slices
- 1/4 cup low-fat evaporated milk
- 1 tbsp whole-wheat flour
- 1/4 cup strong cheddar cheese, grated
- 1/2 lb. wild salmon fillets, cut into 1 1/2-inch pieces
- 1/8 tsp kosher salt
- 1/4 tsp white pepper
- 1 tbsp fresh dill, chopped

Directions:

1. In a large pot over medium-high heat, whisk together the chicken broth, water, carrots, and potato. Bring the soup to a boil while stirring. Once the soup starts to boil, lower the heat to medium and simmer for 10 to 15 minutes, or until the vegetables are tender. Stir at regular intervals to prevent burning. Add the mushrooms.

2. Whisk together the evaporated milk and flour in a small glass bowl to form a lump-free paste. Pour the paste into the soup and bring the soup to a boil while stirring. Bring the soup back to a simmer over lower heat and stir in the cheese until it is properly incorporated into the soup.

3. Over medium-low heat, add the salmon and cook for 3-4 minutes until the fish is completely opaque and flaky. Remove the pot from the heat and stir in the salt and pepper.

4. Pour the soup into bowls and garnish with fresh dill before serving hot.

Prep	Portion	Cook	Per Serving
15 m	8	28 m	*Calories 133; Fat 7g; Sat Fat: 1.3g; Carb 13g; Protein: 5g*

SPICY TOMATO SOUP

- 2 medium yellow onions, thinly sliced
- 3 tbsp extra virgin olive oil
- Sea salt, to taste
- 1 tsp ground cumin
- ½ tsp red pepper flakes, crushed
- 1 28-ounce can of low-sodium plum tomatoes with their juice
- ½ cup crumbled cottage cheese
- 3 tsp curry powder
- 1 tsp ground coriander
- 1 15-ounce can of low-sodium diced tomatoes with juice
- 5½ cups low-sodium vegetable broth

Directions:

1. Place a large wok over medium-low heat and add the olive oil, onions, and 1 tsp salt.

2. Cook for about 12 minutes, stirring occasionally.

3. Add the curry powder, coriander, cumin and red pepper flakes and sauté for about 1 minute.

4. Add the broth and all the tomatoes with their juice and simmer for about 15 minutes.

5. Remove from the heat and blend the soup with an immersion blender until smooth.

6. Serve immediately with the ricotta cheese.

Serving tip: Serve with mozzarella sticks.

Substitution tip: The cottage cheese can be substituted with feta cheese.

Prep	**Portion**	**Cook**	**Per Serving**
15 m	6	3 h	Calories 388; Fat18g; Sat Fat: 5.6g; Carb 45g; Protein: 29g

PORK AND BEAN STEW

- 2 tbsp extra virgin olive oil
- 1 lb. pork shoulder, cut into large pieces
- 1 medium shallot, diced
- 1 tbsp kosher salt
- 2 whole bay leaves
- 1 1/2 tsp ground coriander
- 1 small ham hock
- 1 kg canned northern beans, drained and rinsed
- 1/4 cup canned crushed tomatoes
- 1 1/2 tsp of chili paste
- 6 whole garlic cloves, peeled
- 1 large carrot, cut into rounds
- 1 kg. Portuguese sausage, left whole
- 1/4 cup fresh parsley, chopped

Directions:

1. Preheat the oven to 300°F, with the rack in the center.
2. Heat olive oil in a large, oven-safe pot over medium-high heat. When the oil is hot, fry the pork for a few minutes on each side until evenly browned. Transfer the browned pork to a bowl and set aside.
3. Sauté the shallots in the same pot for about 5 minutes, or until translucent. Return the cooked pork to the pot and stir in the salt, bay leaf, cilantro, and ham hock. Add the beans and tomatoes and stir to mix everything.
4. Add enough water to the pot to submerge the pork to about an inch. Stir while bringing the water to a boil. When the water begins to boil, cover the pot. Place the pot in the oven until the beans have softened (about 90 minutes).
5. Add the chili paste, garlic, carrots, and sausage. Cover the pot again and bake until the carrots are fork tender, about another 30 minutes.
6. Remove the pot from the oven. Take out the sausage and carefully slice it into semi-thick rounds, then stir them into the stew. Cover the stew and return it to the oven for another 10 minutes.

Place the pot on a wooden cutting board and let the stew cool for 10 minutes before pouring into bowls and garnishing it with parsley. Serve immediately.

Prep	**Portion**	**Cook**	**Per Serving**
10 m	6	20 m	Calories 145; Fat 4g; Sodium 261mg; Carb 21g; Fiber 4.7g; Sugar 3.5g; Protein 8g

TUSCAN VEGGIE SOUP

- 1 (15-ounce) can of low-sodium cannellini beans (drained and rinsed)
- 1 tbsp. extra-virgin olive oil
- ½ large onion, diced
- 2 carrots, diced
- 2 celery stalks, diced
- 1 small zucchini, diced
- 1 garlic clove, minced
- 1 tbsp. fresh thyme leaves, chopped
- 2 tsp. fresh sage, chopped
- ½ tsp. salt
- ¼ tsp. freshly ground black pepper
- 32 ounces low-sodium chicken broth
- 14 ounces diced tomatoes, unsalted
- 2 cups spinach leaves, chopped
- ⅓ cup Parmesan cheese, freshly grated, to serve

Directions:

1. Take a small bowl and add half of the beans. Mash them up using the back of a spoon. Set them aside.
2. Place a large soup pot over medium-high heat.
3. Add the oil and let it heat through. Add the carrots, onion, garlic, celery, zucchini, thyme, ½ tsp. salt, sage, ¼ tsp. pepper, and cook for 15 minutes until the vegetables are tender.
4. Add the broth and tomatoes (with their juice) and bring to a boil.
5. Add the beans (either mashed or whole) and spinach.
6. Cook for 3 minutes until the spinach is wilted. Serve with a garnish of Parmesan cheese.
7. Enjoy!

Tip: Serve with grilled baguette slices.

Ingredient Tip: Add chili for a spicier result.

Vegetarian Meals

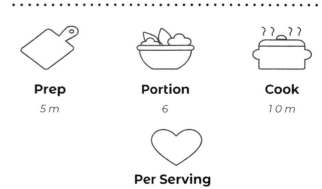

CRISPY VEGGIE PIZZA

Prep
5 m

Portion
6

Cook
10 m

Per Serving
Calories: 324; Total fat: 15g; Saturated fat: 6g; Carb: 30g;
Protein: 16g; Sodium: 704 mg; Fiber: 5g

Ingredients:
1 yellow summer squash, cut into 1/2-inch slices lengthwise
1 small zucchini, cut into 1/2-inch slices lengthwise
1 large sweet red bell pepper, pitted, seeded, and sliced
1 medium shallot, thinly sliced
2 tbsp. garlic-flavored olive oil
1/2 tsp. Sea salt
1/4 tsp. white pepper
1 precooked, 12-inch, thin whole wheat pizza crust
3 tbsp. roasted minced garlic in a jar
2 cups part-skim mozzarella cheese
1/3 cup chopped fresh basil

Directions:
1.   Place all vegetables in a large bowl, and toss with the oil, salt, and pepper until all vegetables are evenly coated.
2.   Heat a large grill pan over medium heat and grill the covered vegetables for 5 minutes, turning halfway through cooking.
3.   Place the pizza crust on a cutting board and spread the garlic over the crust in an even layer. Top with the roasted vegetables and sprinkle with the cheese.
4.   Place the pizza in a heated skillet over medium heat, and grill covered for 5-7 minutes, or until the cheese bubbles and the base is crispy.
5.   Garnish with basil leaves before cutting and serve warm.

Prep	Portion	Cook	Per Serving
10 m	4	5 m	Calories 40; Fat 3; Sat Fat: 0.4; Carb 2g; Protein: 1g

SPICY ZUCCHINI

- 4 zucchini, cut into half-inch pieces
- 1 cup water
- ½ tsp Italian seasoning
- ½ tsp red pepper flakes
- 1 tsp minced garlic
- 1 tbsp extra virgin olive oil
- ½ can of crushed tomatoes
- Sea salt, to taste

Directions:

1. Add the water and zucchini to the Instant Pot.
2. Close the pot with the lid and cook on High for 2 minutes.
3. When finished, release the pressure using the quick release. Remove the lid.
4. Drain the zucchini well and clean the Instant Pot.
5. Add the oil to the Instant Pot and set the Sauté mode.
6. Add garlic and sauté for 30 seconds.
7. Add the remaining ingredients and stir well. Cook for 2-3 minutes.
8. Serve and enjoy.

Serving tip: Serve over rice.

Substitution tip: Add chili pepper for a spicier dish.

Prep	Portion	Cook	Per Serving
5 m	4	35 m	Calories 542; Fat 12; Sat Fat: 2.7; Carb 86g; Protein: 24g

VEGETARIAN PAELLA

- 3 tbsp hot water
- 8 strands of fresh saffron
- 3 cups vegetable broth
- 1 tbsp avocado oil
- 1 large shallot, thinly sliced
- 4 tbsp crushed garlic
- 1 red bell pepper, thinly sliced
- 1 tsp kosher salt
- 1/2 tsp freshly ground black pepper
- 2 tbsp tomato paste
- 3/4 cup canned tomatoes, crushed
- 1 1/2 tbsp smoked sweet paprika
- 1 cup uncooked white rice
- 15 oz. canned chickpeas, drained and rinsed
- 1 1/2 cups haricot verts, cut and split in half
- 1 lime, cut into wedges, for serving

Directions:

1. Gently stir the hot water and saffron in a small glass bowl. Let stand on the counter while you prepare the rest of the dish.
2. Bring vegetable broth to a boil in a medium saucepan over medium-high heat. Once the broth begins to simmer, lower the heat to maintain a very gentle simmer.
3. Heat the avocado oil in a large skillet over medium-high heat. Add the scallions and sauté for about 5 minutes until softened and translucent. Add the garlic and stir-fry for another 30 seconds, so the flavors blend. Add the peppers and continue stir-frying for about 7 minutes until the peppers are tender. Add the saffron with its soaking water, salt, pepper, tomato paste, crushed tomatoes, and smoked sweet paprika, stirring to combine.
4. Add the hot broth, uncooked rice, chickpeas, and haricot verts. When the mixture begins to simmer over medium-high heat, lower the heat and simmer with the lid off the pan for about 20 minutes, or until the rice is cooked and the liquid has reduced.

Suggestion tip: Distribute the cooked rice and vegetables to bowls and serve hot with lime wedges on the side.

Prep	Portion	Cook	Per Serving
10 m	2	18 m	Calories 308; Fat 21; Sat Fat: 3.1; Carb 26g; Protein: 8g

VEGGIE CAKE

- ½ cup chopped white onion
- 1 cup chopped spinach, fresh
- ¼ cup chopped kalamata olives
- 1 tsp. chopped garlic
- 2 tbsp. chopped sun-dried tomatoes
- 1 ½ tsp. chopped walnuts
- ¼ cup whole-wheat flour
- 1 small parsnip, grated
- ¼ cup artichoke hearts
- ¼ tsp. sea salt
- ¼ tsp. ground black pepper
- 2 tbsp. extra virgin olive oil, divided
- 1 small egg, beaten

Directions

1. Take a medium skillet, place it over medium heat, add oil, and when hot, add onion and garlic and cook for 3 minutes until softened.
2. Add spinach, cook for 5 minutes until wilted, transfer the mixture into a large bowl, and set it aside to cool at room temperature.
3. When cooled, add flour, egg, parsnip, artichoke, olives, tomato, salt, and black pepper, stir until well combined, and then shape the mixture into evenly sized patties.
4. Take a medium skillet, place it over medium heat, add oil, and when hot, place the prepared patties and cook for 4 to 5 minutes per side until golden brown.
5. When done, place it on a serving plate, and serve.

Prep

10 m

Portion

4

Cook

6 m

Per Serving

Calories 237; Fat 8.3g; Sodium 521mg; Carb 36.3g; Fiber 5.5g; Sugar 2.8g; Protein 5.9g

PARMESAN POTATOES

- 2 pounds potatoes, rinsed and cut into pieces
- 2 tbsp. grated Parmesan cheese
- 2 tbsp. of olive oil
- ½ tsp. of parsley
- ½ tsp. of Italian seasoning
- 1 tsp. minced garlic
- 1 cup vegetable broth
- ½ tsp. salt

Directions:

1. Add all ingredients except cheese to an Instant Pot and mix well.
2. Seal the pot with the lid and cook high for 6 minutes.
3. Once done, release the pressure using the quick release.
4. Remove the lid.
5. Add parmesan cheese and stir until melted.
6. Serve and enjoy.

Ingredient Tip: Garnish with fresh chopped parsley.

Substitution Tip: Feel free to add other toppings of your choice.

Prep

10 m

Portion

6

Cook

10 m

Per Serving

Calories: 386; Total fat: 12g; Saturated fat: 2g; Carb: 54g; Protein: 16g; Sodium: 732 mg; Fiber: 9g

CURRIED CHICKPEA BURGERS

- 1/4 cup fat-free red wine vinaigrette
- 1 medium shallot, thinly sliced
- 1/4 cup fresh parsley
- 1/4 cup panko breadcrumbs
- 1/3 cup lightly toasted walnuts, chopped
- 15 ounces canned chickpeas, drained and rinsed
- 1/2 tsp. white pepper
- 1 tsp. curry powder
- 1 tsp. turmeric powder
- 2 large free-range eggs
- 2 tbsp. French mustard
- 1/3 cup fat-free mayonnaise
- 6 hamburger buns with sesame seeds, split and toasted
- 6 romaine lettuce leaves
- 3 tbsp. fresh basil leaves, lightly chopped

Directions:

1. Set the oven to preheat to 375degreesF, with the rack in the top third of the oven. Lightly coat a baking sheet with baking spray.
2. Place vinaigrette in a shallow bowl and dip shallot slices. Set aside.
3. Pulse the parsley, bread crumbs, walnuts, and chickpeas on high speed in a food processor until all ingredients are well combined. Add the pepper, curry powder, turmeric, and eggs, before pulsing again until there are no more lumps.
4. Form the mixture into 6 patties about the same size and place them on the prepared baking sheet. Bake the patties for 10-15 minutes or until cooked through.
5. Whisk together the mustard and mayonnaise in a small glass bowl. Spread the mixture on the open sides of each sandwich.
6. Place a single lettuce leaf on one side of each sandwich and top with the soaked scallions. Add a cooked bun to each bun and garnish with the basil leaves before closing the burgers and serving hot.

Prep	Portion	Cook	Per Serving
10 m	6	20 m	Calories 107; Fat 8; Sat Fat: 1.1g; Carb 6g; Protein: 5g

BAKED MUSHROOMS AND TOMATOES

- 2 pounds mushrooms, washed and dried with a paper towel
- 1 cup of red wine
- ½ cup extra-virgin olive oil
- 3 tomatoes, sliced
- ¼ tsp salt
- 1 tsp dried oregano

Directions:

1. preheat the oven to 400°F.
2. Place mushrooms in a baking dish.
3. Add olive oil, oregano, wine, and salt. Mix well and bake for about 20 minutes.
4. Add the seasoning.
5. Serve.

Suggestion tips: Add more dried herbs of your liking.

Prep	Portion	Cook	Per Serving
10 m	2	15 m	Calories 244; Sat Fat 2g; Total Fat: 17g; Protein: 7g; Carbohydrates:27 g; Fiber 13g; Ca 64mg; K 719mg; Na 892mg

ARTICHOKE AND FRESH MINT RISOTTO

- 4 cups vegetable broth
- 4 tbsp avocado oil (divided)
- 1 small shallot, diced
- 4 oz. sweet peas, chopped and halved
- 14 oz. canned artichoke hearts, drained and cut into quarters
- 1 ½ cup Arborio rice
- ¼ tbsp sea salt
- ½ tsp white pepper
- ¼ cup fresh mint leaves, chopped
- ¼ cup fresh chives, chopped
- ⅓ cup fresh flat-leaf parsley, chopped
- ½ lemon, squeezed

Directions

1. Bring the broth to a gentle boil in a large pot over medium heat. When the stock has heated, transfer the pot to a wooden cutting board while preparing the rest of the dish.
2. In a large skillet over medium heat; heat 2 tbsp of oil. When the oil is hot, sauté the shallots, peas, and artichoke hearts, stirring, until the hearts soften and the shallots turn transparent about 6 to 8 minutes. Scrape the vegetables into a small bowl and keep warm.
3. In the same skillet, add the rest of the avocado oil over medium heat. When the oil is hot, sauté the rice and salt, stirring continuously for 2-3 minutes. Don't be alarmed if the rice starts to crackle, pop, and pop-it's normal. Add 1 cup of heated broth to the pan and stir-fry for 5-8 minutes, or until all the liquid has been absorbed. Continue adding 1 cup of broth at a time and cook the risotto until all the broth has been used up or the rice has reached the desired level of tenderness. If all the broth has been used up and the rice is still not quite tender, add water and continue cooking, using ⅓ cup of hot water at a time.
4. Pour the cooked rice into a large serving bowl and stir in the pepper, mint leaves, chives, parsley, and lemon juice.
5. Serve the hot vegetables on a bed of mint risotto.

Notes.

....

....

....

....

Prep
10 m

Portion
2

Cook
30 m

Per Serving

Calories: 324 calories; Fat: 21 g; Sat. Fat: 4.4 g; Carb: 27.1 g; Protein: 9.2 g; Fiber: 6.6 g

STUFFED EGGPLANTS

- 1 medium eggplant, halved
- ¼ cup chopped parsley
- 2 large basil leaves, fresh
- 1 tsp. minced garlic
- ¾ cup whole-wheat breadcrumbs
- ¼ tsp. salt and more if needed
- ¼ tsp. ground black pepper, divided
- ½ tsp. capers
- 1 tbsp. olive oil, divided
- ¾ cup tomato sauce, divided
- 1 medium egg, beaten
- ¼ cup grated Parmesan cheese, low-fat

Directions

1. Turn on the oven, set it to 190 degrees C or 375 degrees F, and let it preheat.
2. Meanwhile, place the eggplant on a cutting board, remove the inside of the eggplant and chop it, and add it to a bowl; set the eggplant shells aside until needed.
3. Take a medium saucepan, place it over medium heat, add ½ tbsp. of oil and when hot, add the chopped eggplant and cook for 3 to 4 minutes until softened.
4. Add the garlic, continue cooking for 3 minutes, transfer the mixture to a bowl, add the salt and black pepper, and stir until mixed.
5. Place the eggplant shells on a cutting board, and then sprinkle with salt and black pepper.
6. Take a medium skillet, place it over medium heat, add the remaining oil, and when hot, place the eggplant shells in it and cook for 5 minutes or more until golden brown.
7. Meanwhile, add the bread crumbs to the eggplant mixture, stir until well combined, add the Parmesan cheese, egg, parsley, and capers, and stir until well combined.
8. Transfer the eggplant shells to a cutting board, and then pour the prepared eggplant mixture into the eggplant shells until stuffed.
9. Take an ovenproof dish, spread some tomato sauce on its bottom, and then place the prepared eggplant shells in it.
10. Add the tomato sauce to the eggplant, scatter basil leaves on top, sprinkle with Parmesan cheese, and then bake for 15 minutes until the top turns golden brown.
11. Serve immediately.

Prep
10 m

Portion
6

Cook
10 m

Per Serving

Calories 44; Fat 3; Sat Fat: 0.3; Carb 4g; Protein: 2g

MEDITERRANEAN-STYLE SAUTÉED BLACK CABBAGE

- 12 cups black cabbage, chopped
- 2 tbsp lemon juice
- 1 tbsp extra virgin olive oil
- 1 tbsp chopped garlic
- 1 tsp soy sauce
- Sea salt and black pepper, to taste

Directions:

1. Add a steaming insert to a saucepan.
2. Fill the saucepan with water to the bottom of the steaming insert.
3. Cover and bring the water to a boil over medium-high heat.
4. Add the black cabbage to the steaming insert and cook for 7-8 minutes.
5. Add the lemon juice, olive oil, garlic, salt, soy sauce, and black pepper to a large bowl. Mix well.
6. Add the steamed cabbage, mix well, and serve.

Serving tip: Serve the cabbage alone or add it to a bowl of cereal.

Substitution tip: Add chili pepper to spice up the dish.

Prep	**Portion**	**Cook**	**Per Serving**
10 m	4	0 m	Calories 41; Fat 0g; Sat Fat: 0g; Carb 9g; Protein: 2g

CUCUMBER AND TOMATO SALAD

- Salt and black pepper, to taste
- 1 tbsp. fresh lemon juice
- 1 onion, chopped
- 1 cucumber, peeled and diced
- 2 tomatoes, chopped
- 4 cups spinach

Directions:

1. Mix the onions, cucumbers, and tomatoes in a salad bowl.
2. Season with pepper and salt to taste.
3. Add lemon juice and toss well.
4. Add spinach, toss to coat, serve and enjoy.

Tip: Top with feta cheese and chickpeas.

Ingredient Tip: Remove seeds from cucumber if you don't want it to be bitter.

Prep	**Portion**	**Cook**	**Per Serving**
10 m	4	30 m	Calories 126; Fat 7g; Sodium 188mg; Carb 14g; Fiber 5.2g; Sugar 3.1g; Protein 6g

BRUSSELS SPROUTS AND PISTACHIOS

1 pound Brussels sprouts, cut and halved lengthwise

4 shallots, peeled and sliced in quarters

½ cup roasted pistachios, chopped

½ lemon, peeled and squeezed

¼ tsp. fine sea salt

¼ tsp. black pepper

1 tbsp. olive oil

Directions:

1. Preheat oven to 400F. Line a baking sheet with aluminum foil.
2. In a bowl, sauté the shallots and Brussels sprouts in olive oil. Make sure the sprouts are well coated.
3. Season with salt and pepper before spreading them on the baking sheet.
4. Bake for 15 minutes. The greens should be slightly caramelized and tender.
5. Remove the baking sheet from the oven and toss the sprouts with the lemon zest, lemon juice, and pistachios.
6. Serve and enjoy!

Tip: Serve with lime wedges on the side.

Ingredient Tip: When sprouts are cooked, add pomegranate seeds, if desired.

Prep	**Portion**	**Cook**	**Per Serving**
5 m	2	2 m	Calories: 398; Fat: 12.2g; Sat fat: 2g; Carb: 56.4g; Fiber: 1.1g; Sugar: 0g; Protein: 12.7g

SICILIAN PESTO GNOCCHI

- 1 cup grilled vegetables, chopped
- 2 cups gnocchi
- 2 tbsp. red pesto
- ¼ cup pecorino cheese
- ½ cup basil leaves

Directions:

1. Boil water in a large pot, add a little salt and add the gnocchi.
2. Cook the gnocchi for 2 minutes and then drain carefully.
3. Return the gnocchi to the pot and add a splash of water.
4. Add the grilled vegetables, basil leaves, and red pesto.
5. Add the pecorino cheese and serve immediately.

Serving tip: Serve with a side salad.

Substitution tip: Pecorino cheese can be substituted for Parmesan cheese.

Prep
10 m

Portion
2

Cook
15 m

Per Serving
Calories: 225.7 calories; Fat: 10 g; Sat. Fat: 1.4 g; Carb: 28.5 g; Protein: 5.7 g; Fiber: 1.4 g

CASHEW SAUCE MARGHERITA PIZZA

- ¼ cup cashews, soaked
- ½ tsp. minced garlic
- 6 leaves of basil, fresh
- ½ tsp. whole-wheat flour
- 1 medium whole-wheat pizza dough, thawed if frozen
- ¼ tsp. salt, divided
- ¼ tsp. ground black pepper
- ¼ tsp. onion powder, divided
- ¼ tsp. garlic powder
- ¼ tsp. dried thyme
- ½ tsp. dried oregano
- 1 tsp. olive oil, divided
- 3 tbsp. tomato paste
- ¼ tsp. miso
- ½ tsp. lemon juice
- ½ cup water, divided

Directions

1. Switch on the oven, set it to 225 degrees C or 435 degrees F, and let it preheat.
2. Meanwhile, take a baking tray, line it with parchment paper, and set it aside until required.
3. Plug in a blender, add cashews, flour, garlic powder, salt, onion powder, miso, pour in water, oil, lemon juice, and pulse until smooth.
4. Take a small skillet, place it over medium heat, add the blended cashew mixture, cook for 3 minutes until thickened and set it aside until required.
5. Take a medium bowl, add tomato paste, oil, onion powder, thyme, oregano, garlic, water, salt, and black pepper, and stir until combined.
6. Place the pizza dough on the prepared baking tray, spread it with your oily finger, and then spread the tomato paste mixture on top, leaving ½-inch of edge.
7. Place spoonful of the prepared cashew sauce all over the pizza, sprinkle basil leaves on top and then bake for 10 to 15 minutes, or until sides turn golden.
8. Cut the pizza into slices and serve.

Ingredient Tip: Add mozzarella cheese on the top.

Prep
10 m

Portion
2

Cook
15 m

Per Serving
Calories: 317 calories; Fat: 14.3 g; Sat. Fat: 4.9 g; Carb: 34.5 g; Protein: 16.2 g; Fiber: 7.4 g

COUSCOUS WITH FETA CHEESE

- 2 cups sliced green lettuce
- ¼ cup shredded cucumber
- 5 ounces chopped spinach, fresh or thawed if frozen
- 2 tbsp. chopped red onion
- 2 tbsp. chopped dill, fresh
- ¼ cup whole-wheat couscous
- ¼ tsp. salt
- ¼ tsp. ground black pepper
- ⅛ tsp. garlic powder, divided
- 1 tbsp. olive oil, divided
- ¼ cup low-fat yogurt
- ¼ cup tofu silken, mashed
- ¼ cup crumbled feta cheese
- ½ cup water

Directions

1. Take a small pot, place it on medium heat, pour in the water, and add the couscous.
2. Cover the pot with its lid, remove it from the heat, let the couscous sit for 5 minutes and then stir it with a fork.
3. Prepare the yogurt sauce and for that, take a small bowl, put the yogurt in it, add the cucumber, garlic powder, and salt, stir until mixed, and set aside until needed.
4. Take a medium bowl, place the tofu in it, add the spinach, onion, feta cheese, black pepper, garlic powder, dill, and couscous, mix until well combined, and form the mixture evenly into four patties.
5. Take a large skillet, put it over medium heat, add the oil and when hot, add the prepared patties and cook for 3 to 4 minutes per side until golden brown.
6. Then place the prepared patties on a serving platter, add the lettuce to the sides, pour the prepared yogurt sauce on top, and serve.

Substitution Tip: You can replace feta cheese with goat cheese

Prep	Portion	Cook	Per Serving
10 m	4	30 m	Calories 307; Fat 12; Sat Fat: 1.9; Carb 46g; Protein: 6g

POTATO AND BEAN SOUP

- 1 1/2 cups water
- 1/4 tsp garlic salt
- 3/4 cup brown basmati rice
- 3 tbsp extra virgin avocado oil (divided)
- 1 large yam, peeled and diced
- 1 medium shallot, finely chopped
- 4 cups spinach, stalkless
- 15 oz. canned turtle beans, drained and rinsed
- 2 tbsp. sweet chili sauce
- lemon wedges for serving

Directions:

1. In a large pot over medium-high heat, bring the water, garlic salt, and rice to a boil. When the water begins to boil, lower the heat and cook the rice with a lid until tender, about 15-20 minutes. Transfer the pot to a wooden cutting board and let the rice rest for 5 minutes.

2. In a large skillet over medium-high heat, heat 2 tbsp of avocado oil. Add the sweet potatoes when the oil is hot and saute for about 8 minutes. Add the scallions and sauté for another 4 to 6 minutes, or until the potatoes are fork tender. Add the spinach and cook until the leaves wilt (about 3-5 minutes). Stir in the beans until heated through.

3. Add remaining oil and sweet chili sauce, stirring to combine. Add the contents of the pan to the cooked rice and stir.

4. Distribute rice and beans to bowls and serve with lemon wedges on the side.

Prep	Portion	Cook	Per Serving
10 m	4	25 m	Calories 108; Fat 9; Sat Fat: 2.1; Carb 5g; Protein: 3g

CURRIED CAULIFLOWER

- 2 tbsp extra virgin olive oil
- ½ cauliflower, cut into florets
- ¼ tsp salt
- 1 tsp curry paste
- 1 cup unsweetened coconut milk
- ¼ cup fresh cilantro, chopped
- 1 tbsp of lime juice

Directions:

1. Sauté cauliflower in heated olive oil over medium heat for 10 minutes.
2. Mix coconut milk and curry powder, add to cauliflower and simmer for ten minutes.
3. Add the lime juice and cilantro and mix well.
4. Serve and enjoy!

Serving tip: Garnish with chives and serve over hot rice.
Substitution tip: Use black pepper for a more vibrant taste.

Prep	Portion	Cook	Per Serving
10 m	6	1 h	Calories 181; Fat 8; Sat Fat: 4.8; Carb 17g; Protein: 11g

CASSEROLE OF WHITE BEANS, ZUCCHINI AND SQUASH

- 1 small butternut squash
- 1 tsp freshly ground black pepper
- 1/2 tsp kosher salt
- 1 tsp chopped dried oregano
- 1 tsp crushed garlic
- 1 tbsp freshly squeezed lemon juice
- 1 tbsp nutritional yeast
- 1 tbsp Extra virgin olive oil
- 8 oz. canned tomato sauce
- 1/4 medium shallot, diced
- 1 medium zucchini, diced
- 2 cups frozen lima beans, thawed
- 4 oz. Swiss goat cheese, grated
- Fresh cilantro leaves for garnish

Directions:

1. Preheat the oven to 375°F, with the rack in the center. Coat a large casserole dish with olive oil spray.

2. Using a fork, poke small holes all over the skin of the squash. Cut off the ends of the squash and cut it in half lengthwise. Discard the seeds before microwaving at a high temperature for 1 minute. Remove the skin and cut the pumpkin into bite-sized cubes. Transfer the cubes to a large bowl.

3. Add the pepper, salt, oregano, garlic, lemon juice, baking powder, 1 tsp olive oil, tomato sauce, scallions, zucchini, and lima beans to the bowl, stirring to combine.

4. Stir in the cheese. Pour the mixture into the prepared casserole dish. Cover the casserole with foil and place in the oven for 30 to 40 minutes, until the cheese and sauce are bubbly and the vegetables are fork tender.

When cooked, garnish with chopped cilantro leaves and drizzle with a few splashes of olive oil before serving hot.

Prep
10 m

Portion
4

Cook
15 m

Per Serving
Calories: 619; Total fat: 31g; Saturated fat: 8g; Carb: 70g; Protein: 21g; Sodium: 113mg; Fiber: 4g

PASTA SARDA

- 1 pound fusilli
- 1/3 cup avocado oil
- 1/4 tsp. white pepper
- 1/2 tsp. lemon zest, finely grated
- 1 tbsp. freshly squeezed lemon juice
- 3 tbsp. crushed garlic
- 2 cups fresh mint leaves, chopped (more for garnish)
- 1/4 cup almond slivers
- 1/2 cup ricotta Salata, grated (more for garnish)

Directions:

1. Cook fusilli in salted water, according to package directions.
2. Meanwhile, puree the avocado oil, pepper, zest, lemon juice, garlic, mint leaves, and almond slivers on high speed in a food processor until lump-free. Add 1/2 cup of the cheese and give it a couple of pulses until all the ingredients are well combined.
3. Once the pasta is cooked, drain a colander over the sink. Transfer to a serving bowl, and scrape the sauce from the food processor over the cooked pasta. Stir gently to combine. Garnish with mint and extra cheese before serving warm.

Prep
5 m

Portion
4

Cook
20 m

Per Serving
Calories 402; Fat 23; Sat Fat: 2.7g; Carb 10g; Protein: 24g

HALLOUMI

- 2 tbsp extra virgin olive oil
- 2 packages of halloumi cheese
- 1 cup of water
- 1/2 cup coconut milk
- 1/4 cup tomato paste
- 1/4 tsp white pepper
- 1/2 tsp ground turmeric
- 1 1/2 tsp curry powder
- 1/2 tsp garlic powder
- 1 tsp onion powder
- 1 small cauliflower, cut into small florets
- ½ tsp Kosher salt
- 2 tbsp coconut flour
- Chopped fresh coriander leaves for serving
- Cooked rice for serving

Directions:

1. In a large skillet over medium-high heat, heat olive oil. Cut the halloumi into 8 slices about 1 inch thick. When the oil is hot, add the halloumi to the pan. You can work in several rounds if you cannot get all of the cheese into the pan. Fry the halloumi on all sides until golden brown. Do not worry if the cheese is difficult to turn at first; it will become easier the crispier the outer coating. Transfer to a serving plate and keep warm.
2. In the same pan, stir the water, coconut milk, tomato paste, pepper, turmeric, curry powder, garlic powder, and onion powder. When the sauce starts to boil, add the cauliflower florets and salt to taste. Simmer the florets for 7-10 minutes with the lid on the pan or until the cauliflower is fork tender.
3. When the cauliflower is tender, add the coconut flour to the skillet and stir until the sauce thickens. Add the cooked halloumi until heated through.
4. Plate the curried halloumi with the sauce and rice of your choice. Garnish with the cilantro leaves and serve hot.

Prep
10 m

Portion
4

Cook
1 h 30 m

Per Serving
Calories 418; Fat 18.5g; Sodium 331mg; Carb 58.6g; Fiber 9g; Sugar 4.3g; Protein 7g

GREEK-STYLE POTATOES

- ⅓ cup olive oil.
- 2 cloves garlic, minced
- 1 1/2 cups water
- Salt and black pepper, to taste
- ¼ cup lemon juice
- 1 tsp. rosemary
- 1 tsp. thyme
- 2 cups chicken broth
- 6 potatoes, cut into pieces

Directions:

1. Place potatoes in a baking dish.
2. Mix all ingredients in a large bowl and pour over potatoes.
3. Bake in preheated 350degreesF oven for 90 minutes.
4. Serve and enjoy.

**Serving tip: Serve with tomato sauce.
Substitution Tip: Use 1 tsp. of smoky, spicy paprika for more flavor.**

Dessert

MEDITERRANEAN-STYLE BROWNIE

Prep
10 m

Makes
8

Cook
20 m

Per Serving

Calories 200; Fat 4.5g; Sodium 87mg; Carb 8.7g; Fiber 2.4g; Sugar 6.5g; Protein 4.3g

Ingredients:

30 ounces canned lentils, rinsed and drained
1 tbsp. honey
1 banana, peeled and chopped
½ tsp. baking soda
4 tbsp. almond butter
2 tbsp. cocoa powder
Cooking spray

Directions:

1.   Preheat oven to 375degreesF.
2.   In a food processor, combine the lentils with the honey and the other ingredients except for the cooking spray and pulse well.
3.   Pour the mixture into a baking dish greased with cooking spray, making sure to distribute the mixture evenly—Bake in the preheated oven for 20 minutes.
4.   Cut out the brownies and serve cold.

Tip: Top with a scoop of your favorite ice cream.

Ingredient Tip: Use aluminum-free baking powder for better taste.

Prep	Portion	Cook	Per Serving
5 m	8	35 m	Calories 215; Fat 16g; Sat Fat: 6.1g; Carb 9g; Protein: 6g

LOW-CARB LEMON CAKE

- Whites of 6 large eggs
- Yolks of 6 large eggs
- Fine zest of 2 lemons
- 1 tbsp freshly squeezed lemon juice
- 1/3 cup coconut oil, melted
- 1 tbsp pure vanilla essence
- Low-carb sweetener to taste (optional)
- 1 tsp baking soda
- 1/4 cup collagen powder
- 1/2 cup coconut flour
- 2 cups almond flour
- 1/2 cup unsweetened large coconut flakes
- 1/4 cup low-fat cream cheese
- 1 cup whipping cream
- 1/2 tsp vanilla powder

Directions:

1. Preheat the oven to 285°F, with a rack in the center. Line a large rimmed baking sheet with greaseproof paper.

2. Beat egg whites with a hand mixer until peaks form. Whisk together the egg yolks, lemon zest, lemon juice, melted coconut oil, and vanilla essence in a separate bowl. Whisk together the optional low-carb sweetener, baking soda, collagen powder, coconut flour, and almond flour in a third separate bowl.

3. Whisk the flour mixture into the bowl of egg yolk mixture

until the batter is lump-free. An offset spatula gently folds the stiff egg whites into the batter. Never stir.

4. Pour the batter into the prepared baking dish in an even layer. Place the pan in the oven and bake until the center is firm and the top well browned about 35 to 40 minutes. Allow the cake to cool completely before adding the top layer.

5. While the cake cools, preheat the oven to 350°F, placing the rack in the top third of the oven. Arrange the fanned coconut flakes in an even layer on a dry baking sheet. Bake for 2-3 minutes, until the flakes are nicely toasted. Set the sheet aside on the counter to cool.

6. In a large bowl, beat the cream cheese, whipping cream and vanilla powder until light and fluffy with stiff peaks.

7. Spread the topping over the cooled cake and garnish with the toasted coconut flakes before serving. Tip: Coconut flakes tend to soften when stored in the refrigerator. If you intend to store the cake and want the flakes to remain crisp, add them to each slice only before serving. The cake can be stored in the refrigerator for up to 5 days in an airtight container or frozen for no more than 3 months.

Prep	Portion	Cook	Per Serving
10 m	2	0 m	Calories: 225; Total fat: 3g; Saturated fat: 2g; Carb: 36g; Protein: 4g; Sodium: 57 mg

HOMEMADE FROZEN VANILLA GREEK YOGURT

- 3 cups low-fat Greek yogurt
- 1 1/2 tsp. pure vanilla essence
- 3/4 cup fine white sugar
- 1 tbsp. freshly squeezed lemon juice
- 1 tbsp. cold water
- 1 tsp. unflavored gelatin

Directions:

Spoon the yogurt into a large coffee filter placed inside a colander or sieve. Place strainer or sieve with yogurt over a bowl; chill covered for 2-4 hours.

2. Once the yogurt is well chilled, scrape the contents of the strainer into a clean bowl and discard the strained liquid. Whisk the vanilla and sugar into the strained yogurt until all the sugar granules have disappeared.

3. Whisk the cold water and lemon juice in a small glass bowl. Gently pour the gelatin over the water and set it aside to bloom on the counter for 1 minute. Place the bowl in the microwave at high temperature for 30 seconds before whisking with a fork. Let stand again for 1 minute or until the gelatin is fully incorporated. Cool for a few minutes before whisking the gelatin

mixture into the yogurt. Cover the bowl and chill for 40 minutes.

4. Scrape the cooled yogurt into a store-bought ice cream freezer and follow the package instructions to freeze the yogurt.

5. Scrape yogurt into an airtight container, and freeze for a few hours until firm enough to scoop out. Enjoy.

Substitution Tip: You can replace vanilla essence with other essences.

Prep	Makes	Freeze	Per Serving
10 m	8	4 h	Calories: 56; Fat: 4.6g; Sat fat: 4g; Carb: 3.9g; Fiber: 1.2g; Sugar: 2.5g; Protein: 0.7g

STRAWBERRY POPSICLES

- 2½ cups strawberries
- ½ cup of almond milk

Directions:

1. Wash the strawberries with cold water and remove the skins.

2. Blend the strawberries and almond milk in a food processor until smooth.

3. Place mixture into stick molds and freeze for 4 hours.

Ingredient Tip: Serve with low-fat yogurt.

Substitution Tip: Almond milk can be substituted for any milk.

Prep
15 m

Portion
4

Cook
40 m

Per Serving
Calories 320; Fat 23g; Sat Fat: 5.1g; Carb 26g; Protein: 2g

LEMON CAKE (GLUTEN-FREE)

- 1 cup almond flour
- ⅔ tsp. baking powder
- ¼ tsp. salt
- 1 large egg, at room temperature
- 7 tbsp. butter, unsalted, softened
- ½ cup coconut sugar
- ½ cup coconut powdered sugar
- ¼ tsp. vanilla extract, unsweetened
- ¼ cup polenta
- 1 tbsp. lemon juice
- 1 tbsp. lemon zest

Directions

1. Switch on the oven, set the temperature to 180 degrees C or 350 degrees F, and preheat.

2. Meanwhile, take a 9-inch pan, line it with parchment paper, grease it with oil, and set it aside until required.

3. Take a medium bowl, place flour and polenta in it, add baking powder and salt, and stir until well combined.

4. Take a separate medium bowl, place butter in it, add coconut sugar and then whisk with an electric hand mixer for 3 minutes until smooth.

5. Beat in ¼ cup flour mixture into the butter mixture at medium speed, beat in egg until incorporated, and then use a spatula to stir in lemon zest and vanilla extract until just mixed.

6. Beat the mixture again until well combined, spoon it into the prepared pan and then bake for 40 minutes until firm and the top turns golden brown.

7. When done, transfer the prepared cake to a wiring rack, and let it cool at room temperature.

8. Meanwhile, take a small saucepan, place it over low heat, add lemon juice and powdered sugar, and cook until sugar has dissolved while stirring constantly.

9. When done, remove the saucepan from the heat, drizzle the prepared syrup on top of the cake and let it cool completely.

10. Cut the cake into slices and then serve.

Prep
10 m

Portion
12

Cook
1h 15 m

Per Serving
Calories 432; Fat 29g; Sat Fat: 7.9g; Carb 39g; Protein: 8g

PISTACHIO AND HONEY BAKLAVA

- Fine zest of 1/2 lemon
- 3/4 cup water
- 1/2 cup raw honey
- 16 oz. frozen phyllo sheets, thawed
- 1 tsp ground cinnamon
- 1/4 tsp ground nutmeg
- 1/3 tsp ground ginger
- 2 cups chopped, lightly toasted walnuts
- 2 cups chopped pistachios
- 1/2 lb. unsalted butter, melted

Directions:

1. Preheat the oven to 325°F, with the rack in the center. Butter a large rimmed baking dish.

2. Whisk together the lemon zest, water, and honey in a small saucepan over medium-high heat. Bring the mixture to a slight boil while continuing to whisk. Lower the heat to maintain a gentle simmer and cook for 25 minutes, stirring at regular intervals and keeping an eye on the heat to prevent burning. Transfer the pot to a potholder and let the mixture cool on the counter while you prepare the rest of the dish.

3. Cut 40 sheets of phyllo to fit the size of your buttered baking dish.

4. In a medium-sized bowl combine the cinnamon, nutmeg, ginger, walnuts, and pistachios.

5. Place a sheet of phyllo in the prepared baking dish and, using a basting brush, coat the sheet with the melted butter. Repeat until you have ten layers of buttered phyllo sheets in the baking dish—Spread 3/4 cup of spiced nuts over the buttered sheets in an even layer.

6. Add 5 more layers of buttered sheets on top of the nuts and sprinkle with 3/4 cup of spiced nuts. Repeat the process of the 5 layers and 3/4 cup until 4 layers are formed. Finally, end the layers with 10 buttered sheets of phyllo dough.

7. With a sharp knife, slice the phyllo dough layers into 1.5 x 13-inch strips. Cut each strip into a rectangle, corner to corner diagonally.

8. Place the baking sheet in the oven for 1 hour and 15 minutes. The dough should be golden brown and crisp.

9. Pour the honey mixture over the hot baklava and let it cool completely on the counter.

10. Serve once cooled.

Prep	Makes	Cook	Per Serving
10 m	24	30 m	Calories 174; Fat 8.2g; Sodium 125mg; Carb 25.2g; Fiber 11g; Sugar 5g; Protein 1.7g

BANANA CHOCOLATE SQUARES

- 2/3 cup white sugar.
- ¾ cup cashew butter
- 2/3 cup brown sugar
- 1 beaten egg
- 1 tsp. vanilla extract
- 1 cup mashed banana
- 1¾ cup flour
- 2 tsp. baking powder
- ½ tsp. salt
- 1 cup semi-sweet chocolate chips
- ½ cup almonds, chopped

Directions:

1. Preheat oven to 350degrees F.
2. In a bowl, add the sugars and butter and beat until lightly colored.
3. Add the egg, mashed banana, and vanilla, then mix well
4. Mix the baking powder, flour, almonds, and salt in another bowl. Add this mixture to the butter mixture.
5. Stir in the chocolate chips.
6. Prepare a baking dish and place the mixture in it.
7. Bake for 20 minutes.
8. Let cool for 5 minutes before cutting into equal-sized squares.

Ingredient Tip: Serve with a hot beverage.

Substitution Tip: Substitute almonds for pecans.

Prep	Portion	Cook	Per Serving
10 m	6	15m	Calories: 405; Total fat: 34g; Carb: 19g; Protein: 8g; Sodium: 70g; Fiber: 4g

RASPBERRY TART IN ALMOND CRUST

- 1/8 tsp. kosher salt
- 1/4 tsp. ground cinnamon
- 1/4 tsp.. nutmeg ground
- 1 tsp. honey
- 3 tsp. unsalted butter, melted
- 1 1/4 cups almond flour
- 1/4 cup dark milk chocolate, chopped
- 8 oz. room temperature cream cheese
- 2 tbsp. amaretto liqueur
- 1 1/2 cups fresh raspberries

Directions:

1. Set oven to preheat to 350degreesF, with rack in center of oven. Lightly coat a large cake pan with baking spray.
2. In a large bowl, whisk together the salt, cinnamon, nutmeg, honey, butter, and almond flour. Use your hands to bring the dough together. Press the dough firmly into the prepared cake pan and bake for 12-15 minutes, or until nicely browned. The edges should just barely lift from the sides of the pan. Allow the crust to cool completely in the pan.
3. When the crust is completely cool, remove it from the pan and place it on a serving plate. Place the chocolate in a small glass bowl and microwave for 1 1/2 minutes, stirring every 30 seconds. Brush the melted chocolate onto the bottom of the crust and half the sides of the edge.
4. Place the cream cheese in a large bowl. Use a hand mixer to beat the cheese for 1 minute, until smooth and lump-free. Gently beat in the amaretto liqueur.
5. Scrape the filling into the prepared crust, and garnish with the fresh raspberries before serving.

Prep	Portion	Cook	Per Serving
10 m	4	1 h	Calories 92; Fat 4.3g; Sodium 55mg; Carb 11.7g; Fiber 2g; Sugar 3g; Protein 2.1g

CRANBERRY AND WALNUT CANTUCCINI

- ¼ cup olive oil
- ¾ cup white sugar
- 2 tsp. vanilla extract
- ½ tsp. almond extract
- 2 eggs
- 1¾ cup all-purpose flour
- ¼ tsp. salt
- 1 tsp. baking powder
- ½ cup dried blueberries
- 1½ cups pistachios

Directions:

1. Preheat the oven to 300degrees F.
2. Mix the olive oil and sugar well in a bowl.
3. Add the eggs and extracts and mix well.
4. Add the baking powder, salt, and flour and mix well.
5. Add the blueberries and walnuts, mixing well to combine.
6. Divide the mixture in half. Form two 12-inch x 2-inch logs and place them on a parchment-lined baking sheet.
7. Place in oven and bake for 35 minutes or until blocks are golden brown.
8. Remove from oven and let cool for about 10 minutes.
9. Set the oven to 275degrees F.
10. Cut the blocks into ¾-inch thick slices and place the slices back on the baking sheet.
11. Bake for 10 minutes or until dry.
12. Serve hot or cold.

Ingredient Tip: Top with your favorite berries.

Substitution Tip: Substitute all-purpose flour for the almond flour.

Prep	Portion	Cook	Per Serving
40 m	2	0 m	Calories 378; Fat 22g; Sat Fat: 6.9g; Carb 49g; Protein: 5g

CHOCOLATE MOUSSE

- 1 medium avocado, peeled, pitted
- 3 tbsp. maple syrup
- 2 small berries
- ¼ cup cocoa powder, unsweetened
- 1 tbsp. almond butter, softened, low-fat
- 1 tsp. mint leaves
- 1 medium banana, chopped
- ½ tsp. vanilla extract. unsweetened
- 2 tbsp. almond milk, unsweetened

Directions

1. Plug in a food processor, add avocado, banana, butter, cocoa powder, vanilla extract, maple syrup, almond milk, and pulse until combined and smooth.

2. Spoon the mousse into a medium bowl, cover with its lid, place it in the refrigerator and let it rest for 30 minutes until chilled.

3. Serve straight away.

Prep	Portion	Cook	Per Serving
10 m	4	10 m	Calories 226; Fat 0g; Sat Fat: 0g; Carb 59g; Protein: 1g

PEACH SORBET

- 2 pounds peaches, pitted and cut into quarters
- 2 cups apple juice
- 1 cup stevia
- 2 tbsp grated lemon peel

Directions:

1. Heat a pan over medium heat, add the apple juice and the rest of the ingredients and boil for 10 minutes.

2. Transfer to a blender and blend.

3. Divide the mixture into small cups and store in the freezer for 2 hours before serving.

Serving tip: Garnish with peach slices and mint leaves.

Substitution tip: Add a tbsp of lemon juice for a spicier taste.

Prep	Makes	Cook	Per Serving
10 m	6	0 m	Calories 184; Fat 8g; Sat Fat: 2.4g; Carb 25g; Protein: 15

FIG AND PISTACHIO CHEESE TRUFFLES

- 1/2 cup dried figs, finely chopped
- 1/2 cup pistachios, unshelled, finely chopped
- 1/4 cup plain cream cheese
- 4 oz. soft, fresh goat cheese
- 1/3 tsp freshly ground black pepper
- 1/8 tsp kosher salt
- 1/8 tsp ground nutmeg
- 1/8 tsp ground cinnamon
- 2 tbsp freshly squeezed lemon juice
- Raw wild honey for sprinkling

Directions:

1. Mix figs and pistachios on a clean baking sheet.

2. Using an immersion blender, beat the cream cheese and goat cheese for a few minutes until well combined and free of lumps. Add the pepper, salt, nutmeg, cinnamon, and lemon juice.

3. Form roughly equal-sized balls and roll them in the pistachios and figs before placing them on a serving plate. Using a fork, lightly drizzle the truffles with the wild honey. If the honey is too thick to drizzle, heat it in the microwave for 10 seconds.

4. Serve the truffles and enjoy.

Prep	Portion	Cook	Per Serving
15 m	2	5 m	Calories 533; Fat 11g; Sat Fat: 4.9g; Carb 99g; Protein: 12

YOGURT AND BERRY TIRAMISÙ

- ¾ cup desired berries, fresh
- 4 small sponge cupcakes, vanilla flavored, low-fat
- ½ tsp. vanilla extract, unsweetened
- 1 cup yogurt, low-fat
- 1 tbsp. brown sugar
- 3 tbsp. cocoa powder, unsweetened
- 2 tbsp. blueberry juice, unsweetened
- ¼ cup water

Directions

1. Take a small pot, place it over low heat, add ¼ cup berries and sugar, pour in the water, and then cook for 5 minutes or more until the sugar has melted.

2. Then remove the pot from heat and let it cool at room temperature.

3. Take a large bowl, place yogurt in it, vanilla extract, and stir until well blended.

4. Take a serving glass, place two cupcakes in it and then top with one-fourth of the prepared berry mixture.

5. Layer the berry mixture with the prepared yogurt mixture, sprinkle with half of the cocoa powder and then layer it with one-fourth of the prepared berry mixture.

6. Assemble another parfait glass in the same manner and then serve.

Prep	Portion	Cook	Per Serving
10 m	6	10 m	Calories 181; Fat 0.5g; Sodium 3mg; Carb 48.1g; Fiber 5.7g; Sugar 39.9g; Protein 0.8g

APPLE WITH HONEY AND CINNAMON

- 6 apples, peeled, cored, and diced
- 1 tsp. of cinnamon
- 1 small orange juice
- ⅛ tsp. nutmeg
- ⅓ cup honey

Directions:

1. Add apples and remaining ingredients to a saucepan, stir well and cook over medium heat.
2. Simmer for 10 minutes.

Serving tip: Stir well and serve hot.

Substitution tip: Add ½ tsp. vanilla extract.

Prep	Portion	Cook	Per Serving
10 m	2	1 h	Calories: 207; Total fat: 17.7g; Saturated fat: 1.9g; Carb: 7.1g; Protein: 7.2g; Fiber: 4.2g

CRUNCHY PISTACHIO COOKIES

- 1 tbsp. finely grated lemon zest
- 1/4 tsp. kosher salt
- 1/2 tsp. powdered nutmeg
- 1/2 tsp. ground cinnamon
- 1/2 tsp. baking soda
- 1/2 cup packaged flax meal
- 2 cups almond flour
- 1 tsp. freshly squeezed lemon juice
- 1 tbsp. pure almond essence
- 2 tbsp. sunflower oil
- 1/2 tsp. pure vanilla essence
- 2 large free-range eggs
- Low-carb sweetener to taste (optional)
- 1/3 cup unsalted, unshelled pistachios

Directions:

1. Set the oven to preheat to 285degreesF, with the rack in the center of the oven. Cover a large baking sheet with parchment paper.
2. In a large bowl, whisk the lemon zest, salt, nutmeg, cinnamon, baking soda, flax meal, and almond flour. Use a wooden spoon to stir in the lemon juice, almond essence, sunflower oil, vanilla essence, eggs, optional sweetener, and pistachios until the mixture just comes together.
3. Use your hands to gather the dough into a smooth ball. Form the dough into a large log that will fit the length of the prepared baking pan— Bake in the oven for about 45 minutes.

Remove the log from the oven and cool on the counter for 15-20 minutes before using a very sharp knife to cut it into 12 equal slices.

4. Lower the oven temperature to 250degreesF. Arrange the slices on the same baking sheet and return the baking sheet to the oven for another 40 minutes. Use a spatula to turn the cookies halfway through the baking time gently.
5. Remove the baking sheet from the oven and let the cookies cool for an hour or two before eating them.

Ingredient Tip: Cookies can be stored in the cupboard in an airtight container for no more than 2 weeks.

Prep	Portion	Cook	Per Serving
10 m	2	50 m	Calories: 153.5 calories; Fat: 12.1 g; Sat. Fat: 7.2 g; Carb: 10.2 g; Protein: 1.2 g; Fiber: 2.2g

CRÈME BRULEE

- 1/3 cup coconut powdered sugar
- 3 tbsp. coconut sugar
- ¼ tsp. vanilla extract, unsweetened
- 2 large eggs, at room temperature
- 1 cup almond cream, low-fat

Directions

1. Switch on the oven, set the temperature to 150 degrees C or 300 degrees F, and preheat.
2. Meanwhile, take a 9 by 13-inch baking pan, place 2 ramekins in it, and set it aside until required.
3. Take a medium pot, place it over medium-high heat, add 1 cup water, bring it to a boil.
4. Take a large bowl, add the egg yolks, whisk until combined, add powdered sugar salt, and whisk until incorporated.
5. Add cream vanilla extract, whisk until well combined, pass the mixture through a strainer into a medium bowl, and divide this mixture evenly between two prepared ramekins.
6. Pour the boiling water around the ramekins in the baking pan and then bake for 45 to 60 minutes until slightly firm.

7. When done, place the ramekins on a wire rack to cool at room temperature, and then refrigerate for 30 minutes.
8. Then place the ramekins on a large plate, sprinkle granulated sugar on top, return the ramekin on the baking tray and broil for 5 minutes until the sugar has caramelized.
9. Then let the brulee ramekins chill in the refrigerator for 30 minutes and then serve.

Prep	Portion	Cook	Per Serving
10 m	4	20 m	Calories 272; Fat 16g; Sodium 84mg; Carb 24g; Fiber 0g; Sugar 20.9g; Protein 6g

VANILLA CUSTARD

- 1 tbsp. cornmeal
- ⅓ cup sugar
- 1 vanilla bean
- 1 cup milk
- 4 egg yolks
- 1 cup of cream

Directions:

1. Cook the vanilla, milk, and cream in a saucepan over medium heat, stirring constantly.

2. Beat the eggs in a large bowl. Add the sugar and cornmeal. Stir well.

3. Add egg mixture to saucepan.

4. Cook until desired thickness is reached, stirring constantly.

5. Serve.

Tip: Serve with chopped fruit of your choice.

Substitution Tip: You may substitute cornmeal for regular flour.

Prep	Makes	Cook	Per Serving
10 m	12	35 m	Calories: 107; Total fat: 7g; Carb: 10g; Protein: 2g; Sodium: 13 mg; Fiber: 3g

CRUNCHY PEARS COVERED WITH WALNUTS

- 1/2 tsp. cinnamon powder
- 1/2 tsp. ground ginger
- 1/2 tsp. ground coriander
- 1/3 tsp. ground nutmeg
- Pinch of salt
- Pinch of freshly ground black pepper
- 1 tsp. ground arrowroot
- 1 tsp. freshly squeezed lemon juice
- 2 tbsp. cold butter, cubed
- 1/4 cup raisins
- 6 small pears, split in half, cored, and sliced (1/4-inch-thick slices)
- 1 tbsp. chia seeds
- 1/2 cup chopped walnuts
- 1/2 cup sliced almonds

Directions:

1. Set oven to preheat to 350degreesF, with rack in center of oven. Coat a large baking sheet with baking spray.

2. In a large bowl, stir together the cinnamon, ginger, cilantro, nutmeg, salt, pepper, arrowroot, lemon juice, butter, raisins, and pears until all ingredients are well combined. Scrape the mixture into the prepared baking dish and spread it in an even layer.

3. stir together the chia seeds, walnuts, and almonds in a clean bowl. Toss the mixture on top of the pears in a single layer.

4. Place the pan in the oven for 35 minutes, or until the top of the crisp is golden brown, and the pears are crispy around the edges.

5. Let the crisp rest on the counter for 10 minutes before serving warm with a topping of your choice, such as vanilla ice cream.

Prep	Portion	Cook	Per Serving
15 m	2	5 m	Calories: 220.1 calories; Fat: 1 g; Sat. Fat: 0.2 g; Carb: 41.3 g; Protein: 4 g; Fiber: 2.5 g

YOGURT AND BERRY TIRAMISÙ

- ¾ cup desired berries, fresh
- 4 small sponge cupcakes, vanilla flavored, low-fat
- 1 tbsp. brown sugar
- 3 tbsp. cocoa powder, unsweetened
- ½ tsp. vanilla extract, unsweetened
- 1 cup yogurt, low-fat
- 2 tbsp. blueberry juice, unsweetened
- ¼ cup water

Directions

1. Take a small pot, place it over low heat, add ¼ cup berries and sugar, pour in the water, and then cook for 5 minutes or more until the sugar has melted.

2. Then remove the pot from heat and let it cool at room temperature.

3. Take a large bowl, place yogurt in it, vanilla extract, and stir until well blended.

4. Take a serving glass, place two cupcakes in it and then top with one-fourth of the prepared berry mixture.

5. Layer the berry mixture with the prepared yogurt mixture, sprinkle with half of the cocoa powder and then layer it with one-fourth of the prepared berry mixture.

6. Assemble another parfait glass in the same manner and then serve.

Prep	Makes	Cook	Per Serving
5 m	9	25 m	Calories 170; Fat 10g; Sat Fat: 2.4g; Carb 16g; Protein: 4g

OLIVE OIL BROWNIES

- ¼ cup extra virgin olive oil
- ¼ cup of Greek yogurt
- ¾ cup of sugar
- 1 tsp vanilla extract
- 2 eggs
- ½ cup flour
- ⅓ cup cocoa powder
- ¼ tsp baking powder
- ¼ tsp salt
- ⅓ cup walnuts, chopped

Directions:

1. Preheat the oven to 350°F and line a baking sheet with paper.
2. Mix the olive oil and sugar in a blender.
3. Add the vanilla extract and mix well.
4. Add the beaten eggs, nuts, and yogurt and mix well.
5. Mix the flour, cocoa powder, salt and baking powder in another bowl and add them to the olive oil mixture.
6. Pour the mixture into the baking dish.
7. Bake for 25 minutes. Allow to cool and cut into squares.

Serving tip: Top with chocolate chips before serving.

Substitution tip: Nuts can be substituted with any other dried fruit.

Prep	Portion	Cook	Per Serving
2 h	4	0 m	Calories 199; Fat 11g; Sat Fat: 4.1g; Carb 16g; Protein: 9g

CHERRY CREAM

- 2 cups cherries, pitted and chopped
- 1 cup almond milk
- ½ cup whipping cream
- 3 eggs, beaten
- ⅓ cup stevia
- 1 tsp of lemon juice
- ½ tsp of vanilla extract

Directions:

1. In a food processor, combine the cherries with the milk and the rest of the ingredients. Mix well.
2. Divide the mixture into small cups and keep it in the refrigerator for 2 hours before serving.

Serving tip: Serve with the cherries.

Substitution tip: You can substitute almond milk for coconut milk.

Prep	Portion	Cook	Per Serving
20 m	5	20 m	Calories 323; Fat 14g; Sat Fat: 2.5g; Carb 42g; Protein: 8g

STRAWBERRY YOGURT MUFFINS

- 1 tsp balsamic vinegar
- ¾ cup fresh strawberries, hulled and roughly chopped
- 1 tsp white sugar
- ¾ cup whole-wheat flour
- ½ tbsp baking powder
- ¼ tsp salt
- 4 tbsp extra virgin olive oil
- ¾ cup low-fat Greek yogurt
- ¼ tsp almond extract
- Pinch of black pepper
- ¾ cup whole wheat flour
- ¼ tsp baking soda
- ¼ cup brown sugar
- 1 egg
- 1 tsp vanilla extract

Directions:

1. Preheat the oven to 390°F and line a muffin tin.
2. Mix the strawberries, white sugar, vinegar, and black pepper in a glass bowl.
3. Cover the bowl and set aside for 1 hour.
4. Add the flours, baking soda, baking powder, and salt to a large bowl and mix well with a wire whisk.
5. In another bowl, thoroughly mix brown sugar with olive oil and egg until well combined.
6. Stir in the yogurt, almond extract, and vanilla extract.
7. Incorporate the yogurt mixture into flour and gently incorporate the strawberries.
8. Spread the mixture evenly into the prepared ramekins in the muffin pan.
9. Bake for 20 minutes.
10. Allow to cool slightly on a wire rack, and then invert the muffins onto a serving plate.

Serving tip: Serve with more strawberries.

Substitution tip: Cinnamon can also be added.

Prep
5 m

Servings
4

Cook
0 m

Per Serving
Calories 309; Fat 14g; Sat Fat: 2.3g; Carb 25g; Protein: 23g

PEANUT BUTTER YOGURT BOWL

- 4 cups vanilla Greek yogurt
- 2 bananas, sliced
- ¼ cup creamy peanut butter
- ¼ cup flaxseed meal
- 1 tsp nutmeg

Directions:

1. Divide yogurt among 4 bowls and add banana slices.
2. Heat the peanut butter in the microwave for 30-40 seconds and add it to the bananas.
3. Sprinkle the flaxseed meal over the top.

Serving tip: Add nutmeg before serving.
Substitution tip: The banana can be substituted with berries.

Prep
10 m

Portion
4

Cook
3 m

Per Serving
Calories 68; Fat 3g; Sat Fat: 0g; Carb 11g; Protein: 3g

COCONUT RICE PUDDING

- ½ cup rice
- ¼ cup shredded coconut
- 3 tbsp of Swerve
- 1½ cups water
- 14 ounces of coconut milk
- A pinch of sea salt

Directions:

1. Spray the inside of the Instant Pot with cooking spray.
2. Add all ingredients to the inner pot and mix well.
3. Close the pot with the lid and cook on High for 3 minutes.
4. When finished, allow pressure to release naturally for 10 minutes. Then release the remaining pressure using quick release.
5. Remove the lid.
6. Serve and enjoy.

Serving tip: Serve with a sprinkling of cinnamon powder.
Substitution tip: Add cardamom for a more intense flavor.

Prep
5 m

Portion
4

Cook
10 m

Per Serving
Calories 171; Fat 8g; Sat Fat: 4.1g; Carb 12g; Protein: 10g

SPANISH VANILLA CREAM

- 1 1/4 cups unsweetened almond milk (divided)
- 1 tbsp unflavored gelatin powder
- 1 1/4 cups whole, heavy whipping cream
- Yolks of 3 large eggs
- 1 tsp ground cinnamon
- 1/3 tsp ground nutmeg
- 1 tbsp pure vanilla essence
- Whites of 3 large eggs
- 1/2 oz. white chocolate, grated
- Low-carbohydrate sweetener to taste (optional)

Directions:

1. Pour 1/2 cup almond milk into a glass bowl and pour gelatin over it. Set the bowl aside to flourish on the counter while you prepare the rest of the dish.
2. Whisk together the remaining almond milk, whipping cream, and egg yolks in a medium-sized glass bowl. Place the bowl over a pot of boiling water. Water should not be in contact with the bottom of the bowl. Gently whisk the mixture over the boiling water until smooth, thick, and creamy.
3. Remove the glass bowl from the heat and gently stir in the cinnamon, nutmeg, and vanilla. Cover the bowl with plastic wrap. With your hand, gently press the plastic onto the surface of the cream. Place the covered bowl in the refrigerator for 30 minutes to chill. During this time, the cream will firm up.
4. In a medium-sized bowl, whisk the egg whites until stiff. Gently incorporate the egg whites into the cooled cream until well blended. Pour the cream into glass bowls or a cake mold and chill for 3-4 hours until the cream has completely solidified.
5. Before serving, garnish the cream with white chocolate and sprinkle with sweetener if desired.

Substitution tip: use dark chocolate (70%) to replace white chocolate.

Index

CONCLUSIONS

Congratulations on making the healthy choice to change your diet. I hope this book has been valuable, provided you with a comprehensive overview of the Anti-inflammatory diet, and gave you the tools to undertake further research. With the Anti-inflammatory diet, you'll find several beneficial effects on your health, including, but not limited to, improving the appearance of your skin, lowering cholesterol levels, helping to prevent the onset of chronic anti-inflammatory based diseases. And all this in addition to losing weight!

Remember not to undergo any significant lifestyle or dietary changes without consulting your doctor, as there may be contraindications.

The first step to making healthier and smarter choices is to make lifestyle changes through a healthy diet, healthy living, and exercise. Follow the 28-day eating plan in this book and eat more natural, unprocessed foods and less packaged, convenient foods to enjoy good health.

APPEAL FROM THE PUBLISHER

Hello, fantastic reader!
I hope you are enjoying this book.

For a small company like us, getting reviews (especially on Amazon) means the possibility to submit our books for advertising. It also means we can just sell a few copies and have a more meaningful effect on society as a whole. So, every review means a lot to us.

We can't THANK YOU enough for this!

Important Notice: We take customer suggestions seriously. If you have any, please write: info@lizzymcf.com writing in the email object the book's title.

Use the QR code below to download your FREE BONUS.

BAKING INGREDIENT CONVERSIONS

BUTTER

Cups	Grams
1/4 cup	57 grams
1/3 cup	76 grams
1/2 cup	113 grams
1 cup	227 grams

PACKED BROWN SUGAR

Cups	Grams	Ounces
1/4 cup	55 grams	1.9 oz
1/3 cup	73 grams	2.58 oz
1/2 cup	110 grams	3.88 oz
1 cup	220 grams	7.75 oz

ALL-PURPOSE FLOUR \ CONFECTIONER'S SUGAR

Cups	Grams	Ounces
1/8 cup	16 grams	.563 oz
1/4 cup	32 grams	1.13 oz
1/3 cup	43 grams	1.5 oz
1/2 cup	64 grams	2.25 oz
2/3 cup	85 grams	3 oz
3/4 cup	96 grams	3.38 oz
1 cup	128 grams	4.5 oz

GRANULATED SUGAR

Cups	Grams	Ounces
2 tbsp	25 grams	.89 oz
1/4 cup	50 grams	1.78 oz
1/3 cup	67 grams	2.37 oz
1/2 cup	100 grams	3.55 oz
2/3 cup	134 grams	4.73 oz
3/4 cup	150 grams	5.3 oz
1 cup	201 grams	7.1 oz

conversion chart
FOR THE KITCHEN

VOLUME MEASUREMENT CONVERSIONS

Cups	Tablespoons	Teaspoons	Milliliters
		1 tsp	5 ml
1/16 cup	1 tbsp	3 tsp	15 ml
1/8 cup	2 tbsp	6 tsp	30 ml
1/4 cup	4 tbsp	12 tsp	60 ml
1/3 cup	5 1/3 tbsp	16 tsp	80 ml
1/2 cup	8 tbsp	24 tsp	120 ml
2/3 cup	10 2/3 tbsp	32 tsp	160 ml
3/4 cup	12 tbsp	36 tsp	180 ml
1 cup	16 tbsp	48 tsp	240 ml

1 QUART =
2 pints
4 cups
32 ounces
950 ml

1 PINT =
2 cups
16 ounces
480 ml

1 CUP =
16 tbsp
8 ounces
240 ml

1/4 CUP =
4 tbsp
12 tsp
2 ounces
60 ml

1 TBSP =
3 tsp
1/2 ounce
15 ml

COOKING TEMPERATURE CONVERSIONS

Celcius/Centigrade	$F = (C \times 1.8) + 32$
Fahrenheit	$C = (F - 32) \times 0.5556$

Printed in Great Britain
by Amazon

20584448R10059